The Pelee Project

*The Hundleys
from Diane
on our first
visit to Pelee
aug. 9, 2003*

Published by ECW PRESS
2120 Queen Street East, Suite 200, Toronto, Ontario, Canada M4E 1E2

NATIONAL LIBRARY OF CANADA CATALOGUING IN PUBLICATION DATA

Christmas, Jane
The Pelee project: one woman's escape from urban madness / Jane Christmas
ISBN 1-55022-547-2
1. Self-actualization (Psychology) — Case studies. 2. Change (Psychology) — Case studies.
3. Simplicity. 4. Pelee Island (Ont.) — Description and travel. 5. Christmas, Jane. 1.Title.
FC3095.P394Z49 2002   158.1´.092   C2002-902170-7
F1059.P254C48 2002

Editor: Amy Logan
Cover and Text Design: Tania Craan
Production and Typesetting: Mary Bowness
Printing: Transcontinental
Cover photos: Ted Rhodes
Photo credits by chapter: ONE: Meloche Monnex; TWO — SEVEN: Ted Rhodes; EIGHT: Jane
Christmas; NINE — FIFTEEN: Ted; SIXTEEN & SEVENTEEN: Jane; EIGHTEEN — END: Ted.

This book is set in Columbus, La Gioconda and Cezanne

The publication of *The Pelee Project* has been generously supported by the Canada Council, the Ontario Arts Council, and the Government of Canada through the Book Publishing Industry Development Program. Canadä

DISTRIBUTION
CANADA: Stewart House, 195 Allstate Parkway, Markham, ON L3R 4T8

UNITED STATES: Independent Publishers Group, 814 North Franklin Street,
Chicago, Illinois 60610

EUROPE: Turnaround Publisher Services, Unit 3, Olympia Trading Estate,
Coburg Road, Wood Green, London N2Z 6T2

AUSTRALIA AND NEW ZEALAND: Wakefield Press, 1 The Parade West,
Kent Town, South Australia 5071

PRINTED AND BOUND IN CANADA

ECW PRESS
ecwpress.com

The Pelee Project

ONE WOMAN'S ESCAPE FROM URBAN MADNESS

JANE CHRISTMAS

ECW PRESS

To my Dad,
who taught me not to be ashamed
of being a square peg in a round world.

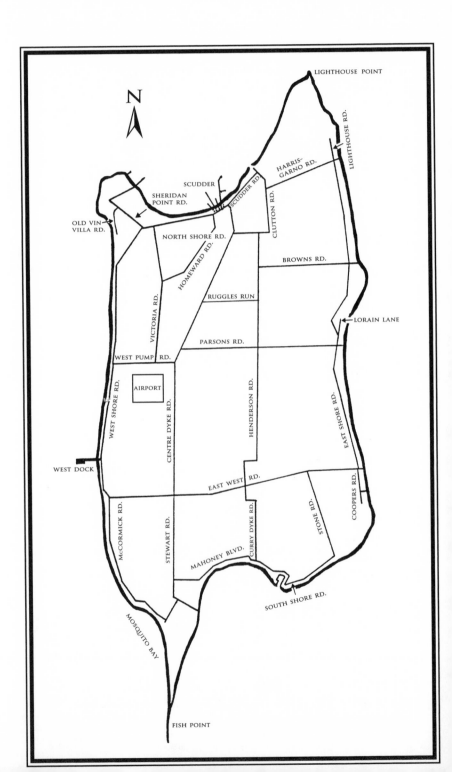

N

LIGHTHOUSE POINT

LIGHTHOUSE RD.

HARRIS-GARNO RD.

SCUDDER

SHERIDAN POINT RD.

SCUDDER RD.

CLUTON RD.

OLD VIN VILLA RD.

NORTH SHORE RD.

HOMEWARD RD.

BROWNS RD.

RUGGLES RUN

LORAIN LANE

VICTORIA RD.

PARSONS RD.

WEST PUMP RD.

AIRPORT

WEST SHORE RD.

CENTRE DYKE RD.

HENDERSON RD.

EAST SHORE RD.

WEST DOCK

EAST WEST RD.

COOPERS RD.

McCORMICK RD.

STEWART RD.

CURRY DYKE RD.

MAHONEY BLVD.

STONE RD.

SOUTH SHORE RD.

MOSQUITO BAY

FISH POINT

Table of Contents

ACKNOWLEDGEMENTS

I could not have written this book without a small, disparate army who helped push this project forward — wittingly and unwittingly. They are, in chronological order: Ted Rhodes, who introduced me to Pelee Island; Ken Whyte and Dianne deFenoyl, who first embraced my Pelee idea and let me run with it; Valeria Grimshaw, who bankrolled my adventure (I paid her back), and continues to love and support me even though I am a difficult daughter; the wonderful people of Pelee Island, who took me and Zoë under their generous wing during the winter of 2001; Allan McGirr and Jennifer Grover, who believe in me and relentlessly encouraged me to turn my newspaper series into a book; the Aspers, who laid me off from my job at the *National Post*, thus freeing up my time to write this book; Jack David, who saw the potential of the rich and untold back story of my Pelee sabbatical and offered to publish it; and Amy Logan, who cheerfully and even-handedly guided the project from start to finish.

Finally, to Adam, Matthew and Zoë, who have been variously impressed and unimpressed by their mother's work: You guys always keep me humble.

Jane Christmas
June 2002

Chapter 1

PEDAL TO MY METTLE

No stop signs, speed limit, nobody's gonna slow me down
— "Highway to Hell" *by AC/DC*

When it comes to defining a chaotic life, a car accident offers a perfect metaphor. After all, it has all the salient buzz terms: losing control, slamming on the brakes, careening from one thing to another, hitting a brick wall. But for some of us, metaphors aren't enough. We need the real thing. On January 13,

2000, I had a car accident that, to this day, amazes me, terrifies me, and oddly enough, fills me with gratitude.

I was on my way to work, a punishing 60-kilometre commute from Hamilton to Toronto. There are various routes into Toronto, each more hellish than the next, but that day I chose Highway 401, a kind of trophy road for veteran commuters: if you can survive the stretch of the 401 that winds like an intestinal tract across the top of Toronto, you can survive just about anything.

My job didn't start until 10 a.m., so I was mercifully spared the full brunt of morning rush-hour traffic. Still, in Toronto at least, a city of more than three million people, there is no beginning or end to rush hour anymore; the highways are a continuous, bumper-to-bumper caravan of cars and trucks at all hours of the day and night. All traffic, all the time. On the days when traffic is lighter, the stakes are jacked up exponentially: speed limits are ignored, and the highway becomes an autobahn, making anyone who travels at 120 k.p.h. feel like a slacker. Push the pedal to 140 clicks, and drivers will still whiz past you like distracted poodles on Dexedrine, snarling at your timidness while simultaneously juggling a coffee, a cellphone, makeup, an upcoming boardroom presentation, the kitchen renovation, and (oh, yes) a steering wheel. It's truly a scary sight. It makes you wonder whether some drivers are even aware they're on a highway.

On that glorious January morning, however, I was only too aware that I was on a highway. But something didn't seem right. The conditions were unnaturally good: it was a sunny day, and the roads appeared to be clear of snow and ice; there wasn't the usual throng of cars on the road, and people were driving slower. What was going on? Where were the road-raged drivers? The speeders? That day, the inexplicable absence of urban madness irritated me. Clear roads, no snow falling, light traffic, slow drivers. What the hell was wrong with everyone? Hadn't their caffeine fixes kicked in? In a fit of characteristic impatience, I clenched my teeth and muttered "Fuck this!" as I floored the gas pedal and prepared to change lanes.

That's when it happened. My car spun suddenly to the left and into a concrete barrier, ricocheted back to the opposite side of the highway, and smashed into a metal barrier. Then it bounced again to the left side of the highway and into a concrete barrier. It didn't stop there: spinning in circles, it looped back to the other side, but now a transport truck, its driver apparently unconcerned about my zig-zagging car, had moved in front of me. I had no choice but to plough into it, and I calculated that decapitation would be quick and clean. I braced myself, closed my eyes, and broadsided the trailer head on. My car spun like a top until it came to a sudden stop on the right shoulder and rammed another highway barrier. I opened my eyes and watched the transport truck amble down the highway: it didn't even stop. Incredibly, I hadn't collided with any other vehicles.

I sat there for a moment in stunned silence, afraid to move, almost afraid to breathe. Blood began to trickle down my face.

My immediate reaction spoke volumes about just where my undecapitated head was at that moment: I extended my right arm, ejected the Madonna tape from the tape deck, and dropped it between the seats: if someone found out I had been listening to Madonna, I thought, I would never live down the shame. Thank God I didn't have AC/DC blaring on the system, although under the circumstances *Highway to Hell* would have been a more fitting soundtrack for my dance with death than "Isla Bonita."

Next I chastised myself. I had spied some inexpensive gas on my drive in and had treated my car to a fill-up. Now here I was with a full tank of gas and a wrecked car. Great. Don't you just hate it when things like that happen?

In the midst of this curious mental discourse, everything suddenly went dark. A tarp had been thrown over my car, and I heard a male voice holler out with words that chill me to this day, "Has anyone checked the body?"

The body? My body? "I'm not dead yet, pal!" I wanted to call out, but I could only muster a groan. A police officer poked his head under the tarp. He looked at me, his eyes widened in surprise, and then he disappeared. "She's alive! Get an ambulance! Quick!" he yelled. If his first words had petrified me, his next words, which he spoke into his radio, made me grin: "Woman, appears to be 30 to 35. . . ."

Lord, love him: his estimate had shaved about 15 years off my age. I was bleeding, I was bruised, God only knew what other injuries I had, but my vanity was in perfect working order. (So, it turned out, was the Madonna tape.)

A crowd gathered around my car. A woman, clearly distraught after witnessing my car's pinball-like performance, offered me her cellphone to call someone. Whom would I call?

My mother? And worry her? One of my ex-husbands? He might be upset that I'd survived. My boyfriend lived in Windsor, but I didn't think it was polite to make a long-distance call on a stranger's phone. A girlfriend? I was sure they were all busy. Frankly, I didn't want to call anyone; I ignored the stinging reality that I really didn't have anyone to call. However, I didn't want to seem ungrateful to this kind woman who'd stopped to offer assistance. Plus, she seemed more upset than I was, so I called my office and calmly told a co-worker I'd had an accident and didn't think I would make it to work that day. That was an understatement.

The scene outside my car had escalated to full-blown emergency mode. I felt I should be helping, but then I was the one who had put us all in this fine mess, so I figured I had better just shut up and behave myself. I glanced down to make sure Madonna was out of sight.

The consensus, it appeared, was unanimous: I shouldn't have survived the accident. The police said so, the paramedics said so. Later, the insurance agent who saw the photograph of my mangled car told me people die in less serious accidents. But not only had I survived the accident, I had walked away from it. On my way to the ambulance, I turned to look back: my black 1997 Honda Civic EX barely resembled a car.

I wanted to cry — from the fear, from the shock, from the loss — but I had been taught to hold back public displays of emotion until a more appropriate time: maintain a stiff upper lip, I had been told. Instead, I found myself trying to put the paramedics at ease as they worked feverishly to get me to a

hospital that wasn't in Mad Hatter mode: "No room! No room!"
I couldn't surrender control to someone else, even to those who
were trying to help me.

It wasn't until a few hours later, when I took a taxi to my
mother's home in Oakville, just west of Toronto, that the
enormity of what had happened struck me. Curled up in the
fetal position on the back seat of the cab, it dawned on me how
a car spinning out of control and crashing into a concrete
barrier was an apt description of my life. This accident was no
accident. It was a sign.

Yet how bad was my life? I wasn't doing drugs, or smoking,
or drinking heavily, or gambling, or carousing all night — not
even part of the night. I wasn't in any destructive or abusive
relationship. I was just a mom with three beautiful children, a
lovely little home, a good job, and a new boyfriend. What was
complicated about that?

As a matter of fact, it was very complicated. Modern life
was making it so. It was always so rushed, so stressful, so
nonstop. It didn't seem like I was on a treadmill — that would
have been a luxury! Instead, it seemed like I was constantly
competing in an urban triathlon with no opportunity to relax
and enjoy what I had. My energies and my loyalties were
stretched to the limit: I was generous and accommodating to
those who really didn't matter, such as bosses and co-workers,
and miserly and miserable with those for whom I cared most.
Having given my all at the office, I short-changed my children
on affection and help with their homework because I was
drained by the end of the day. Every drop of my being had

been wrung out by the time I got home each night.

On really bad days, which seemed to be almost all of them, I would call my children during my drive home and ask them to have a glass of wine ready for me. "Red or white?" they would ask obediently. Pretty savvy for children who were only eight and 13 at the time. Pretty pathetic parenting too. When I reached my driveway and turned off the car, my head would flop against the steering wheel. It was all I could do to drag myself and my various satchels and briefcases out of the car and into my home.

Weekends were no better. All the mundane but necessary chores that hadn't been done during the week were crammed into a two-day window. On Saturday evenings, the time I set aside for my children, I would settle into the sofa with them to watch a movie, only to fall asleep within 10 minutes. Sunday became a race against the clock to get it all done before the Monday-morning alarm.

I had long lost the capacity to listen — really listen — to my children or to anyone; I had perfected a habit of intently looking at people with compassion-filled eyes while simultaneously making a mental list of things I had to pick up at the store. My mind was constantly on the go. Of course, my children could see through the ruse immediately. "Repeat what we just said," they'd command. When I couldn't, they would collapse in tears and accuse me of not loving them. I felt like a fraud.

Friends? Did I still have any? It had been so long since I had seen some of them that I couldn't remember whether our estrangement had been the result of scheduling problems or a falling out. I didn't savour time with my family or friends. Time spent with them just filled the gaps between my next errand, my next chore, my next appointment.

As the days sped by, I found myself playing catch-up with numerous obligations. There was rarely time to sit still and catch my breath, and the more I was deprived of downtime the more I became angry and resentful about the demands placed on me by other people. I had no control over my life. On those rare occasions when I was able to accomplish everything on my list, I felt dissatisfied and anxious. So I made more lists. I made lists of lists. I made pie charts. Then I made pies. I kept a time sheet to see where the day went. Then I had to spend a day to see where my time sheet went.

Everything conspired against my search for a comfortable, well-ordered groove. At one point, I used prayer as a means to calm and focus myself, and it worked. It was my favourite time of the day, but then my job got changed, and so did my hours of work, and all of a sudden prayer time was squeezed out of my packed schedule. When I could no longer fit church services into my life, I sought out psychics to get a bead on who I was and where I was headed: I was truly lost and had mislaid my compass.

It was no surprise that I was rushed; the whole world was rushed. Everyone moved at a ferocious speed while they simultaneously complained that life was too busy. They just threw up their hands and smiled gamely, as if to say, "Hey, what can you do about it?"

Women, in particular, complained of being stressed out and exhausted to the point of tears as they struggled mightily under the weight of daily life and the incessant demands from those around them. Like them, I craved a few quiet moments to collect my thoughts, focus my life, and enjoy a little peace. But the only place they seemed to be able to do that was in the aisles of grocery stores or in the car on the way to pick up a child from hockey practice. Isn't it always the way? Just when you settle on the sofa with a magazine and raise a cup of hot (and fresh) tea to your lips, a child will seize the moment to ask, "Can you sew my pants?" "Can you sign this form?" "Can you read *Macbeth* and help me with my essay? It's due tomorrow."

The search for silence became a bit of a competition among several of my friends. After a weekend, we'd compare notes on our Quest for Quiet and swoon with envy when one of us boasted of having had *four straight hours* of uninterrupted solitude. Quiet time, we nodded gravely, was definitely more important than sex.

The antidote to fast living appeared in the form of magazines and books that began sprouting up. There was talk of the New Simplicity, and people began shedding their possessions as speedily as they could organize garage sales to dispose of them. Predictably, many of these people took their garage sale winnings and bought a new image for themselves that superficially replicated a simpler, less cluttered life. Simplicity was being packaged, revised, and abridged for millennial appeal: soothing pictures (lots of creamy white decors), pat solutions, and platitudes. It bugged me that simple living had been reduced to a marketing niche cloaked in a semiglossy magazine (not a completely glossy magazine, which wouldn't look simple). When one such magazine held court on how to organize an underwear drawer, I figured the New Simplicity had created a cult of simpletons. I didn't want to *read* about the New Simplicity. I wanted to live and breathe it.

In her book *Simple Abundance*, Sarah Ban Breathnach wisely comments on the parallel universes of abundance and lack, and the struggle we confront each day over which one to inhabit. People have never become wealthy spending time with their children or caring for their homes, but such things create a sense of abundance that can't be measured on a ledger. I could relate to that. Unfortunately, I couldn't relate to the *Simple Abundance* plan itself — it seemed too much like work. And it didn't seem to address a deeper need.

My world was steeped in sadness. In 15 years, I'd had eight jobs, seven homes, three children, two marriages, two divorces, two step-children, and a recently deceased parent. It felt more like eightjobssevenhomesthreechildrentwomarriagestwodivorces-twostepchildrenandarecentlydeceasedparent. What was in store for the next 15 years? More of the same? Forget it! I was already tapped out.

When I looked beyond my own life, the social landscape wasn't much better. Marriages were breaking up, friends were breaking down, children were caught in the middle, people were losing their jobs, their homes, their children, their parents. Couples I had over for dinner one week were in court with each other the next. People I spoke to one day were dead the next.

Against this maelstrom, I tried to pull together an oasis in my home to at least mimic tranquillity. It worked for a while, but you can manufacture serenity for only so long. My home *looked* lovely and orderly, but my life resembled the Gaza Strip — sniping, bickering, days of simmering hostilities, and then back to open warfare after dinner. My father was dying, my mother was crying, my kids were fighting, my ex-husbands were opening old wounds. Friends sought advice from me on their own crises, and I obligingly added their baggage to my overloaded luggage cart. I had a new man in my life, but I had no idea where or how he would fit in. The phone never stopped ringing, people never stopped wanting something from me. And I never felt like I was doing enough, even though just about every hour of my day was accounted for. Through it all, I was consumed with trying to improve myself. What could I do to be a gentler mother, a more caring friend, a more tolerant ex-wife, a better daughter, a more valued employee?

Naturally, such rigorous self-improvement always came last on my to-do list. Things that directly affected me or that I could do for myself were always placed last. Everything had to be perfect before I could tend to myself. No wonder my life felt so overloaded: it was easier to sort the laundry than to address a personal sea-change.

Women often put off taking care of themselves in order to tend to others. That's admirable, really it is, but there is a time and a place for it. When we routinely put our needs at the bottom of the list, we devalue ourselves to the point where we are worth less than the Canadian dollar. How many of us have just wanted to put our feet up and read but were nagged by the thought "Oh, just let me vacuum the house first, and then I'll relax"? I often played a perverse game of delayed gratification with myself. I refused to allow myself the treat of doing the crossword or doing my nails until I had finished at least 15 items on my 25-item list. And that was just the morning.

Men, I found, seem to juggle things more easily. Perhaps they are more comfortable with delegating things, or maybe they just avoid or ignore the domestic details of life. I asked my boyfriend, Ted, about this. He is a single father with financial obligations that stretch him to the breaking point, yet many times he would regale me over the phone about his latest squash game or his dip in the whirlpool at his club.

Impressed but suspicious, I asked him, "Don't you have laundry to do or house cleaning? What about your kids?"

He had all of those, he admitted. But there were certain times for all of them. "Besides," he pointed out, "I'm not a psycho house-cleaner, like you."

I chuckled good-naturedly and immediately lumped Ted in with the majority of men who manage a fine balance because they are unashamedly selfish — not in a bad sense but in the sense that they don't have a problem putting themselves at the top of the list when the situation warrants it.

But that's not a woman's way, it certainly wasn't my way. And in time I reaped the dubious reward of trying to be all things to all people: I developed back and shoulder muscles that stung with pain when anyone touched them.

The field of intuitive healing links certain physical disorders with emotional tribulations. In essence, your biography begets your biology. Dr. Caroline Myss, in her remarkably enlightening book *Anatomy of the Spirit*, attributes those tense back and shoulder muscles to misaligned issues involving grief, resentment, trust, and loneliness. Likewise, Myss theorizes that breast lumps and breast cancer indicate hurt, sorrow, and unfinished emotional business connected to nurturing; varicose veins relate to people's inability to stand up for themselves; obstetrical and gynecological problems are connected to issues of power and control; thyroid and throat problems affect those who struggle with personal expression and decisiveness. It's a fascinating field.

By extension, I saw my car accident as not really an "accident" but an intentional event on the cause-and-effect continuum. People who have been in a serious car accident do not come away from it with knee-slapping enthusiasm. Accidents are so jarring that they literally rattle your bones and shake up your cells. A type of terror is implanted in your brain, and like an echo it engages in an obsessive and random replay of the sequence of events that can last days, weeks, months, and even years. When your mind isn't engaged in reviewing the choreography of the crash, it is incessantly analysing the cause. Was it a mechanical failure? A confluence of scientific principles? Some wayward physical presence — a stone perhaps — that threw the car off course and triggered the accident? Was it human error? Was it simply meant to be?

My car accident knocked some sense into me. Like Marley's ghost appearing on Scrooge's door knocker, it made me conscious of the need to change and to stop behaving like a self-indulgent Boomer brat.

There was also something about the accident that concerned

me more than the bruises on my face and chest and the swelling around my eyes. When my car was ricocheting across the highway, it really felt as if a hand was throwing it around. This force, whatever it was, didn't want me to die — just to wake up. I was completely aware of that while I was in the car, which probably accounts for why I addressed the Madonna in my tape deck before I addressed the Madonna in the sky in the first moments after the crash. While I instinctively knew I wasn't going to die, I understood I was being given one heck of a lesson. It was like being grabbed by the shoulders and told, "Get a grip! Wake up and smell the burning rubber! Is this what it's going to take to get you to change? Have I got your attention now?"

I knew I had come close to death. I knew I had to stop talking about making lifestyle changes and actually start making them. It was time for action.

So I headed to Holt Renfrew.

Chapter 2

WALK A MILE IN MY MANOLOS

Days! Are you kidding? I don't have days,
I have minutes. Everything is rush!
— Manolo Blahnik

OK, so life-changing decisions should not begin with a new pair of shoes. This wasn't a federal budget, after all. But having spied a pair of Manolo Blahniks on the feet of the Princess of

Wales several years earlier, I had promised myself that, before I died, I would satisfy my inner princess and buy a pair. Since my number had almost come up, I figured I had better move smartly — I doubted that heaven had a shoe store. Besides, how expensive could a pair of shoes be?

About $600. And they weren't the most expensive little puppies in the store either. The day I sashayed into Holt Renfrew on my self-appointed mission, I noticed a pair of Puccis for $1,250. As I saw it, the Blahniks were a bargain.

But this purchase wasn't about money. It was about entitlement. This was payback time for the worry, the stress, the scrimping, the chores, the friends I had consoled, the people who had treated me callously, the bosses who had refused to promote me, the bosses who had fired me, the rejected résumés, the men who had dumped me, the women who had gossiped about me, the grade six teacher who had told me I would never make it to university because I was left-handed, the pissy checkout girl who had rung up an item twice and hadn't apologized for it, the drivers who cut me off in traffic, the banks that charged usurious service fees and had the temerity to call it "service," the times I had cheerfully driven my kids to wherever they had wanted to go, the times I had uncheerfully reprimanded them and spanked them, the countless times I had always made sure to take the smallest cookie on the plate and leave the larger ones for others, the grief I carried over my father's death, the anger I directed at my parents and at myself because I could never measure up to what they wanted me to be. This was one loaded purchase.

A pair of red slingbacks with princess heels did the trick. Without batting an eyelash, I made my purchase and left the store. Did I feel guilty about spending what amounted to more than a month's worth of groceries for my family? No. Ashamed? No. Excited? No. Not even a bit. I felt nothing. I did like the shoes, though. They were lovely and really comfortable. Too comfortable. A few months later, I returned to Holt Renfrew and bought another pair, this time in black.

As I stared into my closet one day, I could not, for the life of me, figure out why, with two pairs of Blahniks now in my closet, I wasn't happy. I was just as overwhelmed and frantic as I was before I bought the shoes. Perhaps I expected those shoes to have the same protective effect as Dorothy's ruby slippers: the Blahniks would shield me from the slings and arrows of outrageous urban life. But they didn't. I felt more vulnerable and more run-down.

Shopping wasn't the answer so I tried a different strategy. I asked my doctor for Prozac, an antidepressant I had been taking for about five years. Depression wasn't new to me; I'd had it since I was a teenager, but it was only in my 40s that the dots were connected and my medical chart was officially stamped "clinical depression."

There is nothing to be ashamed of when you have depression. When you consider depression as a chemical imbalance, which it is, the medication is really just a supplement to replenish your serotonin levels. If you were dehydrated, wouldn't you add water to top up your personal reservoir?

While Prozac was helpful in getting me to a point where

life could be handled a bit more serenely, it only served to mitigate the problem, not solve it. After five years, Prozac just wasn't doing it for me anymore. Still, I went ahead and got the prescription filled.

Referring again to Dr. Caroline Myss's *Anatomy of the Spirit*, I learned that depression is the result of a fragile immune system that can be traced back to social and familial chaos. Hmmm. It was time to dig deeper. Obviously, a high-speed life was exacerbating some deep-seated chaos. Looking back, I realized I had allowed myself to be rushed through major decisions and experiences. Life, like household bills, needs to be processed and deliberately filed. If not, our mental and emotional "paperwork" creates a backlog that sends us into panic. As one psychiatrist told me bluntly, "The reason you feel so overwhelmed is because you *are* overwhelmed. Slow down!" But no amount of medication, short of a lethal injection, was going to help me do that.

I tried to slow down, I really did, but instead of facing the black dog of depression, I faced a black hole. As I delved further into my being, I discovered a gap where my soul was supposed to be parked.

Maybe that was it, I thought. Maybe, over time, my spirit had become disconnected. I wasn't a godless person — I'd always felt a strong connection to God — but I realized my spiritual side, along with other facets of my life, was on autopilot. I was play-acting at living. I knew the words to life, and I could hum the tune, but I didn't really appreciate the music. I had been grazing the surfaces of things for too long, not because I didn't want to dig deeper, but because doing so simply took too much time. Time was something I didn't have. I definitely needed a time-out.

With summer approaching, Ted thought we should rent a cottage for a week. Ted is the type of person who exudes an air of calm. A tall, thin, good-looking man with a thick head of light brown hair flecked with grey, he is an outdoorsy type who moves slowly and never carries a list. He is my polar opposite. Even though ours was a relatively new relationship — and a long-distance one, at that — Ted quickly saw the intensity of my life and the impossibly high standards I set for myself and others. And he wanted nothing to do with it. Whenever I was in the middle of some minor crisis, whenever the flames of hell seemed to be scorching my toes, I would look around and find Ted engrossed in a crossword puzzle, his lanky frame stretched out on my sofa. The man lived for moments like that. I, on the other hand, barely had time to leaf through a newspaper and find the crossword, let alone do one. In fact, the sight of Ted lolling about made me resentful and envious. How come I never had time to lie on *my* sofa? I barely had time to sit on it.

Now Ted was on the phone suggesting a holiday. I had a hard time imagining this guy on a holiday, let alone needing one. He carries himself as if he is always on holiday. What would he do on a holiday anyway, I wondered, two crosswords a day? At least I was certain of one thing: he would never sanction the type of vacation in which you do six cities in six days.

I liked planning trips as much as I liked travelling. (Actually, I liked planning trips because it gave me control over where I would be staying. We perfectionists are demanding when it comes to accommodations.) But this time, I couldn't have cared less. I told Ted I was too tired and too distracted to plan anything. If he would make the arrangements, I would accept what he chose. I did, however, have two stipulations: no outhouses and no wild and crazy nightlife. It had to be a quiet and tranquil destination.

While Ted looked into a holiday off the beaten track, I looked into the stars. My daily horoscope, which I read purely for entertainment (unless it told me something I wanted to hear), warned of a period of great transition: "You find a need to dismantle everything in order to build up something new." I wasn't an architect, so I dismissed the literal interpretation. But if I was, indeed, in a period of transition, how long would it take before I received my new life? A week? A month? OK, two months?

Waiting for my life to change was worse than knowing I had to make a change. I didn't have a clue about which direction I should go or whether I should even change direction. And what about my children? Was I supposed to drag them around with me until I found myself? How responsible was that?

I wanted a change *now*, but I also knew I couldn't rush it; I was only too aware of the results that come from rushing. I decided, instead, to let my chaotic life play itself out a little longer. Yeah, that's what I would do. With luck, it would just burn itself out. Maybe the holiday would give me a break from my routine and a chance to really look at my life. Perhaps that was all I needed.

A week later, Ted called to say he had narrowed our holiday destination to two places: Algonquin Park and Pelee Island. "Which would you prefer?" he asked generously.

All I knew about Algonquin Park was that it was woodsy and way north of Toronto. A vision flashed before me of bumper-to-bumper traffic along a two-lane highway on a stinking-hot July long weekend for what I calculated to be a four-hour drive. I didn't think I could handle that. "Where's Pelee Island?" I asked.

Ted explained that Pelee Island was in the middle of Lake Erie, and we would have to take a ferry from Leamington or Kingsville — he wasn't sure which — to get there.

Leamington? Kingsville? Lake Erie? Where on Earth were those places? Living and working in the Centre of the Universe (in this case, Toronto), everything else was off the radar screen.

Ted, however, lived and worked in Windsor, and he knew the area well. Plus, being an outdoorsman, he could sniff out an unbeaten track easily. He had never heard of Manolo Blahnik before he met me.

I, on the other hand, had never heard of Pelee Island, but based on Ted's description it sounded OK. After all, it would be for only a week, I told myself. I would survive. And if it was a bust, it would simply confirm my insistence on being the one to plan a holiday. Ted would never be allowed to book another vacation for as long as we were together.

So Pelee Island it was. Our ferry departure was booked for July 2, about six weeks away. I wondered whether I could last that long on my own highway to hell.

The Pelee Project

On July 2, I was leaning over the railing of the *Jiimaan*, an enormous ferry, as it sailed out of Leamington harbour bound for Pelee Island.

Our holiday was off to a bad start. My depression — or was it just sadness and emptiness? — had become so bad I started entertaining fantasies about throwing myself overboard. I stared into the frothy bilge below; it was taunting me. I imagined slipping beneath the gentle waves and disappearing forever. I thought of my children — Adam, Matt, and Zoë. Damn. If I jumped, it would really mess up their lives.

I looked over at Ted. The blazing afternoon sun had picked out the grey flecks in his hair and gave it a silvery glow. He was excited about us being away together, but he also knew that my serotonin levels were boring their way to China at that very moment. If I jumped, it would ruin his vacation. Plus, how much of a loser would he feel like, trying to explain to people that he had booked a holiday for his girlfriend and that she had thrown herself overboard at the start of their vacation? The optics certainly didn't look good on that one. There wasn't much chance I would feel better anytime soon either: I had inadvertently left my Prozac at home.

I could sense a mean, bitchy streak welling up inside me. Poor Ted didn't know what he was in for. If he hadn't dumped me by the end of the week, then I would have to book him in for a psychiatric examination: he was either a masochist or an idiot. It never occurred to me that he was simply patient. We stared into the lake in silence.

An hour into the voyage — I had no idea Lake Erie was so big — Pelee Island loomed into view. As the *Jiimaan* glided along Pelee's west side, the island and I surveyed each other warily.

"Hmmm. I don't know whether I'm going to like you," the island seemed to say to me.

"Yeah? Well, consider yourself on probation too," I countered, a little surprised that I was having a telepathic conversation with an island. "I've been all over the world," I added haughtily, "and there are a million more where you came from."

The island retorted with one of those just-you-wait-and-see snickers, and our staring contest continued.

Ted broke in, relieved, I'm sure, that we had completed the passage without him yelling, "Girlfriend overboard!"

"Sooooo, there's the island," he said.

"Yeah, we've met," I said curtly, turning away. Ouch. I made a mental note to be nicer and to try harder.

Ted and I walked down the stairs to the ferry's lower deck, got into our car, and drove off the boat and onto Pelee Island.

A week later, we were back on the *Jiimaan*. My eyes were red, and tears were staining my cheeks. I had fallen madly in love, and I didn't want to leave. The peace, contentment and warmth lavished on me were like nothing I had experienced.

Ted and I had done really well too. He wasn't the least bit offended that the island had gathered me in its arms and monopolized my time.

For the entire week, Pelee and I couldn't get enough of

each other; it flirted with me shamelessly, and I lapped up every bit of it. Our days were spent on sun-drenched sandy beaches, and biking up dirt roads, past tidy vineyards that reminded me of France. The sky was so clear that on some days we could see across the lake to the Ontario mainland. It was such a relief to be away from it. My favourite beach was in the shadow of an old lighthouse that was being restored — a strangely familiar lighthouse, I thought. I kept thinking I had seen it before but of course, that was impossible. I ran on the beach, into Lake Erie's sparkling waters. Was the water clean? Who cared! It was refreshing. As I splashed in the waves, pressed my body against the heat of the sand, explored the tangled woods, and squealed in delight when a bunny scampered across my path, I could feel the island smiling and nodding benign approval.

The natural setting and sights weren't the half of it. Although Pelee had been populated for nearly 200 years, and tourism had been pivotal to its economy for the past 75, I was stunned that the place had escaped the mass franchising of McDonald's, Tim Hortons, and Starbucks. There were no billboards, traffic lights or street lights. It didn't have a bank — not even an instant teller. There were no cutesy shops or attractions that you might expect in such a place, although it did have a fascinating local museum. You couldn't even say Pelee Island had charm in the conventional sense of the word. It had something bigger than that. It had unmanufactured simplicity. What you saw was what you got.

In hindsight, it was an easy and, perhaps, predictable seduction. Pelee and I wanted each other, and we needed one another. But it had lessons to teach me, and for once I was an obedient pupil.

My first lesson took place at Dick's Marina, on the island's south end. Ted wanted to hire someone to take us out to Middle Island, Canada's true southerly point, which had been purchased from private American owners by the federal government in 1999 for $1.9 million. The job of escorting us to Middle Island fell to Lyle, manning the marina's desk that day. Lyle had a slow gait and a severe expression, and he didn't look too happy about being disturbed. But he ambled over to his boat and started the motor nonetheless. I figured he thought we were a couple of stuck-up city slickers, so I worked hard to change his perception. He was a tough nut to crack. He certainly didn't feel compelled to put on a touristy front for us; instead, he kept a stony watch on the sky and the lake.

Tenacious to the point of annoyance, I kept up my banter with Lyle, asking him how long he had lived on Pelee Island. He told me he had been there all his life.

I laughed. "No, really," I said. "How long have you lived here?"

"All my life," he assured me. "I was born here, went to school here, I work here."

"Haven't you ever wanted to move to a big city, like Toronto?"

He looked insulted.

"OK," I said. "How about Windsor or Leamington?"

"Too busy," he said. "It's a rat race over there. Who needs it?"

A rat race in Leamington? Jeez, I thought, that was rich. As for "Who needs it?" wasn't "need" a moot point? Wasn't it everyone's duty to participate in the urban frenzy? Did we even have a choice?

Yet here I was, at the epicentre of unpretentiousness, where such choices were made without guilt or regret. Simplicity was chosen because it was the best choice, and in some cases the only choice, not because it was being heralded across the pages of a magazine that month. At that moment, I saw how easily I had been entranced by the clarion call of city life. It was such a tempting call — the money, the bright lights, the glittering restaurants, the snooty sales clerks — that I had completely forgotten I had the free will to reject it. No one had forced me into a chaotic life; I had simply chosen it. Now I was mired in it. The well-trod path to greener pastures was littered with millions of disillusioned souls, and Lyle had been smart enough to know he would be one of them. It never fails to amaze me how the most important life lessons are taught by the most unlikely people. Lyle had shone a klieg light on the blind obeisance that city people mistake for sophistication.

Lyle let up on the throttle as we approached our destination.

Legend has it that no less a luminary than Al Capone had used Middle Island as an export depot for his bootlegging business. A fabulous mansion had been built there, though few people had actually seen it up close. As luck would have it, our Lyle said he was one of them. As caretaker for the property, he had made numerous forays to Middle Island over the years. The island had its own airstrip and the house possessed richly detailed woodwork and huge fireplaces. Mysteriously, the house burned down in the 1980s. With Middle Island now in Ottawa's hands, the plan was to turn it into a nature reserve.

The island proved to be more inhospitable than Paris on a rainy day. Lyle steered the boat as close to the shore as possible, and suddenly a gazillion cormorants, which had overtaken the island and were devouring the foliage at a rapacious rate, started up a hellish squawking. As Ted started collecting his camera equipment, Lyle warned us that if we took one step out of the boat the cormorants would begin self-induced vomiting and would pelt us with their bile until we left.

Parisians aren't quite that bad, but we got the point. Besides, Lyle was now rolling his eyes upward — and not because I insisted on chattering to him (though maybe he was). The sky had clouded over, and he told us we were heading back to Pelee.

Lake Erie had become choppy, and, as Lyle turned the boat around and gunned it back to Pelee, the spray from the waves flew in my face. Lyle, who had softened a little over the course of our journey, apologized and handed me an old towel lying on the floor of the boat. I thanked him but said the towel wasn't necessary: the spray felt good. I think Lyle thought I was on drugs. Not many city girls appreciate having what amounted to a small bucket of water tossed in their faces every five seconds. Even Ted was taken aback.

My next encounter with Pelee's countercultural ways occurred a few days later.

True to Ted's word, Pelee was low-key, especially at night. We wiled away the evenings hunkered over a Scrabble board locked in deadly competition or played Frustration, some hideous card game Ted had learned. I was losing one night, so I

suggested we go for a drive. I had a sudden craving for a chocolate bar.

"Good luck," Ted said. "I don't think there's anything open,
but we'll try the grocery store."

I looked at my watch. It was 7:30.

We drove into the empty parking lot of the A.M.
McCormick grocery store. A man was on his tractor-mower
cutting the grass. Ted and I walked up to the doors of the store:
it was closed. The man called out to us. "What do you want?" he
asked above the noise of his mower.

We waved back to him and headed back to the car.

The man cut the mower's engine. "Can I help you?"

"Oh, it's OK," Ted answered. "She wanted a chocolate bar,
but the store's closed. Thanks anyway."

"Just walk in," said the man, restarting his mower. "They're
inside stocking the shelves."

We didn't know who "they" were, but we went back to the
doors and opened them.

"The man outside said to come in," I ventured tentatively to
the two women behind the counter, expecting to hear "We're
closed."

Instead, I heard a gentle, almost lyrical, voice say, "It's OK, come
on in."

Ted and I looked at one another.

"I only want a chocolate bar," I said, still standing at the door.

"That's fine," one of them said, barely looking up.

I felt pretty guilty, so we decided to buy more than a chocolate bar. As we were checking out, I thanked the woman again

while she booted up the computerized till. "I suppose you close at seven o'clock," I said. It was now close to 8 p.m.

"No, we close at five," she answered matter-of-factly.

"You close at five, and yet you let me in so I could buy a single chocolate bar?" I asked incredulously.

"Sure, why not? It's not a big deal," she answered, smiling. "Plus, you didn't just buy a single chocolate bar, did you?"

Wow. How many times had I arrived at the doors of an urban store just as it was closing, or arrived minutes before it opened in the morning, and seen the clerks inside pretending to ignore me? What does it take to open a store 10 minutes earlier when people with money in their pockets are lined up outside the door? When did we become a society of such rigid time keepers?

Ted and I left the store and waved good-bye to the nice man on his lawn mower. There was something else that made this store stand out. The clerks hadn't once said "Have a nice day" the way they do in the city as a kind of verbal balm for urban-ites who want a homespun atmosphere while they're ordering a triple mocha frappé and yapping on their cellphones.

The day arrived for Ted and me to leave Pelee Island. I couldn't bear to go.

A few hours before we boarded the ferry, we signed up for a quick tour of the Pelee Island Winery and finished it with a barbecue and a bottle of the local merlot on the winery's patio. It was a hot, brilliantly sunny day, and it's safe to say Ted and I were fairly in the bag by the time we boarded the ferry. Maybe Ted was right: it was the wine that prompted my tears once we stumbled to the upper deck. But I was also truly sad about leaving.

"Let's come back," I said, even before the ferry had pulled away from the dock.

Ted laughed and said we could. He figured I would forget about the island by the time the wine wore off.

But I didn't. Pelee Island was not only my epiphany but also my drug.

When I got home, I told everyone I met about the amazing island where I had spent my holiday. All of them, to a person, had the same response: "Um. Where is Pelee Island, exactly?" No wonder. According to brochures put out by Ontario's Ministry of Tourism, southern Ontario ends at Point Pelee, a spit of land off the northern shore of Lake Erie. Indeed, few Canadian maps, I discovered, showed the full and true boundary of the country: they don't dip low enough to show Pelee Island. As far as Canadians are concerned, their country ends at Point Pelee, on the Ontario mainland. Few are aware that Point Pelee and Pelee Island are two different places.

Back in my urban cesspool, Pelee's magic stayed with me, and I felt the island's tug constantly. Ted and I made a couple of trips over in the fall. Once we visited Pelee just for the day and bicycled around the entire island. Another time I woke my children at 5 a.m. on a Saturday, bundled them into the car, drove three and a half hours to the ferry, and then propped them up for the one-and-a-half-hour passage so they could see my favourite new place. Zoë loved it, Adam thought it was OK, Matt pronounced it "lame." I was obsessed.

Then, during one late-fall weekend visit to the island, as I sat alone at the water's edge watching Zoë clamber over the rocks that formed the breakwater, I searched my brain for an idea that would allow me to live on Pelee Island. I had never wanted anything more in my life — not even my Manolo Blahniks could beat this. My superbusy life had worn me down and sucked me dry. I wanted to be free of the urban trappings. I wanted my soul back.

I knew I wasn't alone in wanting to live a more simple, tranquil life. A quiet movement was afoot. Like me, thousands were clamouring for inner peace and outer sanity as if these intangibles were the Holy Grail. Everyone was talking about the New Simplicity: no less an authority than Oprah was weighing in on the subject. Excess was out; pared-down living was in. But was the New Simplicity a way of life that modern people could really cleave to, or was it just another fad, something to be added to the panoply of experiential living?

I wondered whether I could convince the *National Post,* my employer, to explore the issue in depth and thereby covertly sponsor my spiritual rehab. It was a quirky enough concept for the *Post* to do — it was always sending reporters off on crazy missions. But there was a catch: I was an editor not a reporter, and I was firmly typecast in my role, much against my wishes. But I was desperate and, as Lyle had learned to his sorry detriment, tenacious.

On that dock, I sat down and crafted my pitch to Ken Whyte, the *Post's* editor-in-chief: Take a stressed-out urban mother, drop her on an island over the winter months to test the

New Simplicity, and see if she caves under the weight of culture shock or finds peace. I would tell him that I wanted to be that stressed-out mom — I *was* that stressed-out mom — and that I had picked a little-known Canadian island. (Perfect! Canadian content!) Then I would throw down my trump card: I would go off the company's payroll and freelance the columns. Yeah. That was it! What executive isn't tempted by a cost-saving initiative?

I mulled this over on the long drive back to my urban life. When I arrived home, I e-mailed my proposal to Ken. I felt a pang of terror as I hit the send button.

The next morning, his reply was waiting for me. I held my breath. There was always the chance Ken would say, "Thanks, but I didn't hire you to do this." Or "Good idea. I'll give it to one of our real reporters." But he didn't. He said he liked the idea and asked me to run it by the life editor.

He liked it? I scrolled down to see if the words "just kidding" were somewhere in the note. I immediately forwarded the message to Dianne deFenoyl, the *Post*'s life editor. To ensure she read it promptly, I inserted the golden password in the memo field: "Ken likes this idea."

Ten minutes later, Dianne e-mailed me back. She said she loved the idea, and she was going in to talk to Ken. I looked toward her desk just as she scurried into Ken's office. Five minutes later, she was back at her desk, typing furiously. Within minutes, an e-mail from her arrived. (We could all see each other in the *Post*'s newsroom, and we all had legs, but people rarely spoke to each other there; they converse by e-mail. I once sat in front of a guy who would e-mail me constantly throughout the day. Sometimes he even phoned me. I finally turned around one day and said to him, "You can just call my name, and I'll turn around and talk to you, OK?" He reacted as if I had just suggested a novel form of communication.)

When Dianne's e-mail arrived, I snapped it open. The wheels, it seemed, were already in motion. Dianne and Ken had established a fee for my weekly columns. The series would run for 15 weeks: I would start on January 8 and finish up on Easter weekend.

Three months on Pelee Island. I couldn't believe it. The saying "Be careful what you wish for" sprang to mind.

It was October 24, and I had much to do, a lot to organize, and some big decisions to make. But first I had to tell my family and friends. Their reactions nearly nixed the plan entirely.

Chapter 3

PACKING IT IN

Yesterday went by so quick it seems like it was just today / My
daughter wants to throw the ball but I'm too stressed to play.
— "Rock Bottom" *by Eminem*

As I mapped out my Pelee Island sabbatical, my life entered a more chaotic and fractious phase — if that was possible. The irony wasn't lost on me that attempting simplicity was stressful. I seemed to be a magnet for stress. The preparations, in fact, proved to be about as stressful as the reasons behind my leaving in the first place, and all sorts of emotional barricades and physical impediments were thrown in my path.

There were times when I broke down from the strain of arranging the logistics of my sabbatical and also knowing I was ending a chapter of my life. Do I take the well-worn path that, though not perfect, was at least familiar, or forge an uncharted route and hope that it would lead, if not to nirvana, then to a new understanding and appreciation of life?

It was a critical juncture. Each scenario held a kind of doom; one was unpalatable, the other was unknown. The indecision paralyzed me.

Moving on was not just scary, it was sad. Though the retreat was for only three months, it might as well have been three years. I was bidding adieu to my old life and its familiar surroundings and habits. I was also closing the doors on a few relationships.

At first, I resisted. In some hilariously deluded state, I began to deny that my life had even come off the rails. It didn't seem all that different from other people's lives; in fact, mine looked pretty good. I had everything I wanted, and I was content with most of the decisions I had made in my life. But it was an empty contentment. I needed a change from the relentless pedal-to-the-metal existence. The pressure to push harder and faster, to do more and be more, was killing me. On and on, an internal battle raged. Should I stay, or should I go?

But if life was puzzling, so too was the reaction to the news of my impending retreat. I knew the biggest opposition would come from my family, because the retreat involved making alternative arrangements for my children, and I was dependent on the cooperation of others.

Zoë was firmly on board. As she rationalized it, the chance to have a stay-at-home mom for three months was tantamount to winning the lottery. When she first learned that we were indeed going to Pelee Island, her face displayed a look she normally reserved for Christmas morning. It amazed me that she could so easily trade her extended family, her friends, her toys, her routine, and her school for three months with mom. If nothing else came of the retreat, it would be worth it just to give her that gift.

Adam was curious about the retreat, but I think he was just being diplomatic. He preferred his creature comforts and routines. He had also signed up for house-league hockey at the local arena, and he didn't want to forfeit the opportunity or the deposit. He did appease me by saying he would visit us during March Break.

Matt was a different story. Not only was he not going to join us on Pelee Island, he didn't think I should go. "Why can't you just accept your life the way it is?" he argued. "No one else's mom does this sort of thing." At 15, Matt was at the stage of full-blown teenage rebellion where a craving for change is balanced by a craving for things to stay the same. He wasn't about to give up a thing — for anyone. As he railed against my plan, I tried to reason with him, but it was pointless. I began to wonder which one of us was more rebellious. Adam was already living full time with his dad; now Matt would join them.

Divorced families perform a delicate but complex choreography when it comes to dealing with their children and living arrangements. My situation was no different. Naturally, there were all sorts of objections from various camps within my family and extended family. They all seemed to have the same basic aim: to prevent me from leaving them for three months. At one point, the spiritual component of the retreat became moot for me: I just wanted to get the hell away from everyone.

I received a more positive reaction from Ted, who thought the chance to live on Pelee Island was terrific. But he was already looking beyond the retreat. It was only a short-term remedy to a larger problem, he said. What would happen three months down the line, after the experiment was over, he wondered. My response was, "Who cares what happens three months down the line? I'm doing this *now*. The retreat is a stepping stone, not a solution."

My mother, widowed for nearly two years, saw my Pelee adventure as a great release for me. She, more than anyone perhaps, had seen my life spiral downward from two failed marriages, the stress of raising children as a single parent, and a pressure-cooker job. She knew I felt constantly under the gun. But she also viewed my retreat as a form of abandonment. My father's death, and her recovery from hip and knee surgery, had made her dependent on me to run errands, deal with some of her household crises, and just be there for her. She believed it was my daughterly duty to continue doing so. Instead, I was now telling her she had to take care of her own problems for a few months. She was understandably of mixed emotions.

While the reactions from my family were more or less predictable, I was unprepared for the responses from some of my friends. A few of them were unflinching in their moral support, but others greeted the news as if I had told them I had taken a Doberman pinscher as a lover. They were perplexed about why I had to go to such seemingly drastic lengths. "Oh, God! No Tim Hortons?" they gasped. And why leave at all, they asked. Couldn't I just conduct my spiritual retreat from home, without upsetting the familial applecart? I guess they thought I could telecommute my way to a more balanced life.

I tried to explain to them how important it was to really get away — away from the house, the city, the routine, the conveniences, the phone, the bickering children, the daily obligations that go with being part of a family: I needed a break from the aural environment as well as the physical one. What I didn't tell them was that, if I embarked on a spiritual journey from the comfort of my home, they wouldn't respect my privacy. My sabbatical would turn into a three-month open house.

Some people do not understand solitude; in fact, the very idea frightens them. They equate it with drinking problems and pornographic pursuits. What's more, solitude scares them because it's the pad from which deep, troublesome thoughts launch into consciousness, thoughts they would prefer not to confront.

Then there were the catty friends — now relegated to the rank of ex-friends — who were so mean-spirited I wondered whether I should rethink my plans and make this a permanent move. What was the big deal? I couldn't imagine these people were happy with the person I had become. But, strangely, they were.

_?_?

It wasn't until months later that I partly understood their anger. They were upset about losing the character I had inhabited for years. Many of us unconsciously (sometimes even consciously) create roles for ourselves that fit the scripts or expectations of those in our immediate sphere. In a way, we're all casting directors in the drama of life, and we choose people to fill certain roles in our individual dramas: the mean-spirited ex, the saintly friend, the problematic child, the eccentric parent, the loopy neighbour. When we make changes to ourselves, we inadvertently force those around us to rewrite their scripts. Either they make the necessary adjustments, or they write us out. For instance, if you have a zany, glamorous, jet-setting friend who suddenly announces she's becoming a nun, how will your friend's new persona fit into your life and the circle of characters you have created? Suddenly, that friend may no longer hold much appeal for you, because it was really her glittery aura, her larger-than-life drama, that attracted you.

The same, I discovered, held true for me. It was only when I was miserable and vulnerable that certain people embraced me; when things improved for me or I gained emotional strength, they became distant and critical.

What really ticked them off, it seemed, was not that I had dared to dream but that I had dared to turn dream into reality. Apparently, I hadn't received the heavenly directive informing me that I wasn't supposed to do that. It reminded me of something Bette Midler once said, and it wasn't, paradoxically, "You gotta have friends." In an interview many years ago, she recalled that her friendships had declined proportionately as her

star had risen: "If I had relied on my friends for career encouragement," she revealed, "I'd still be singing in bathhouses." Trust
me, there is no better litmus test to determine your true friends
than telling them you are embarking on a spiritual retreat.

No matter what people said, or how they said it, I refused to
be deterred. I'll admit I was a hag during this transitional
period. I even surprised myself at how scream-till-your-lungs-
bleed stubborn I could be. The more people disapproved, the
more I dug in my princess heels — and the deeper I found
myself in a tunnel of loneliness and isolation. This, too, was a
crucial stage in the departure process. I almost gave up from the
sheer exhaustion of trying to explain myself to everyone or
from the fear of knowing I would be shunned by those people.
But when I broke through this emotional barrier, it was like
passing through a gateway into another realm.

To temporarily divert myself from this cheerful outpouring
of goodwill, I scouted around for a place that Zoë and I could
rent on Pelee Island. The island isn't large, about five kilometres
wide and 15 kilometres from top to bottom, and its population
is small: 2,000 in the summer months, only 150 during the
winter. Consequently, there weren't a lot of winterized houses
to choose from.

There was added urgency to my search: if I expected to
get my car onto the island, I had to do so before ferry season
ended in mid-December — about six weeks away. I threw my
business card around whenever I visited the island and asked
people I met if they knew of a place I could rent. The fact
that I was looking to rent during the winter immediately

placed me on the islanders' suspicious-persons list.

"You want to come here in the winter?" they asked incredulously. "There's nothing here in the winter."

"That's exactly what I want," I replied.

One islander asked quietly if I was running from an ex-husband. "Actually," I whispered back to him, "I'm running from two ex-husbands."

Another islander had a novel idea for securing lodging. "Since you're a writer, and you're from Toronto, why don't you give Peggy a call?"

Peggy?

"Yeah, Peggy. Margaret. Atwood. She has a place here. I'll bet she'd put you up."

I knew two things about Margaret Atwood: I knew she was a formidable writer, and I knew she wasn't the type of person who would gamely put me up — even if I was from Toronto. But the comment did underscore the difference between the Pelee way of life and my urban way of life. Islanders are so accustomed to helping each other (even those they don't particularly like) that it's hard for some of them to comprehend why one person from Toronto wouldn't help another person from Toronto. I made a mental note to check out the Pegster's digs.

One day while I was toiling away in my office cubicle, propping my eyelids open with toothpicks as I edited a story about information technology, I got a call from an islander named Irma. She had heard about my search and offered her home while she vacationed in Florida.

That weekend I sailed out with my children to see the place, a renovated farmhouse that sported new cream-coloured siding. The property was dotted with a number of outbuildings, including a barn, a garage, a garden shed, and an outhouse (whose service, I hoped, had been retired). From a tree limb hung a tire swing.

Irma had turned her home into a B&B to handle the summer's tourist overflow. She had christened it Nothing Fancy "because it isn't," she said resolutely. But it was clean, spacious, and bright with big windows. It didn't have a view of the lake, but as the deadline for my departure neared, I was past being picky. The living room and dining room walls were painted pale pink, and the furniture featured a small formal dining room suite. Upstairs were three large bedrooms. I looked around and thought, "Yup. I think I can do some serious calming down here."

We worked out the rent and my arrival date and then shook hands. Zoë and I now had a place to live on Pelee Island.

A few weeks later, I returned bleary-eyed — yet again — to the Leamington dock to load my car and some belongings onto the ferry. As I drove up to the dock like the weary Pelee veteran I felt I had already become, I found myself face to face with a mesh metal fence and a sign telling me the ferry was leaving from the Kingsville dock. My heart began pounding at twice its rate. I looked at my watch. I had 10 minutes to make it to Kingsville, about 12 kilometres west of Leamington. I tore down the road like a maniac — hey, I had plenty of experience tearing down roads — and squealed onto the Kingsville dock with about a minute to spare.

The ferry was nothing like the big, shiny *Jiimaan* I had sailed on every other time I had visited Pelee. This one looked like a beaten old scow.

"We *are* going to Pelee Island, aren't we?" I asked a deckhand, who looked at me as if to say, "No, sweetheart, we thought we'd shake things up a bit and aim for St. Lucia today."

As I headed into the lounge, giving the boat a quick once over, I spotted Irma. She had decided to make the trip with me to brief me about her home and to introduce me to some of the islanders. "Is this boat safe?" I quietly asked Irma as I slid into the bench across from her. She informed me that the venerable *Pelee Islander* was better than the *Jiimaan*.

Irma and I eased into conversation, and I learned a bit more about her. She had been born on another island — Prince Edward Island — and life had brought her eventually to southern Ontario. She was a widow and a cancer survivor, and, having retired from her job at a nursing home, she had decided to move to Pelee Island for no other reason than to satisfy an urge to live there. She, too, spoke of the irresistible tug of the island.

As I sat speaking with her, gently rocked by the movement of the boat, it occurred to me that it had been ages since I had sat down with anyone and spoken in such a relaxed manner. What's more, I was actually retaining the information. Irma and I spoke at a moderate pace, in a moderate tone, something I hadn't done in my high-octane life, where speaking had become as rushed as pizza delivery.

We could hear — and feel — the boat cutting through the ice as it made its way to Pelee. The crew decided then and there that this would be the last voyage of the season. What luck, I thought: I had managed to get my car over just in time. Usually, when I play Russian roulette with weather and timetables, I lose.

The crew also decided that, since the ice was getting treacherous, the boat would dock at Scudder Dock, the marina at the north end of the island, rather than at the island's usual West Dock terminal. The move would shave about 20 minutes off the voyage.

The two docks are as different as night and day, and perfectly illustrate the concept of free enterprise versus government intervention. Scudder Dock is a long cement pier with the remnants of Pelee's past — a granary and a fishery — still standing proud, albeit weather-beaten. West Dock is all new brick, steel-mesh fences, official-looking ticket wickets, and many signs to enforce regulations. And, of course, it is where the *Jiimaan* can dock (which it can't do for logistical reasons at Scudder Dock). Scudder Dock was in use for more than a century before the government, in its pointy-headed wisdom, decided it was better to throw away millions of taxpayers' dollars to build a dock on the west side that was inconvenient, reoriented the entire island's community, and ensured that people would complain about it for decades. Our tax dollars at work indeed. *oh, come on!*

The *Pelee Islander* pulled into Scudder, the ramp was lowered, and I drove off the ferry, along the narrow pier, and onto Pelee Island. The sun suddenly burst out from behind a cloud, and its warm beams glittered off the snow like diamonds. I could barely contain my excitement. As I dutifully followed Irma's truck down a snow-covered country road, my eyes darted around at landmarks I hadn't noticed on previous trips, and I made a note to check them out once I was there full time. The island looked so different with its trees stripped of foliage and the land blanketed in pure white.

We arrived at Irma's house and unloaded my car. After Irma gave me a quick run-through of the mechanics of the house, I hopped into her truck for a whirlwind tour of the island, though whirlwind was a bit of an understatement: the roads were icy, and Irma had a heavy foot. At one stop sign, she braked abruptly, and her truck went into a 360-degree spin. We looked at each other and started laughing, though this little incident brought back visions of a similar spin on Highway 401 that had landed me here in the first place. So my laugh was more a stiff "hee hee" than a hearty "ha ha."

At the grocery store, I was introduced to Zane, one of the island's old-timers, who, eager to establish his credentials with a newcomer, launched into the history of Pelee's pheasant hunt. Irma waved him off and told him he had all winter to talk to me; we were in a hurry. I thought that was a bit indelicate, so I smiled at Zane and promised him I definitely wanted to hear his stories.

Irma's abruptness, I later discovered, was one of the island's quirky mannerisms. Everyone waved everyone else away like so many flies at a picnic. Extreme niceties just weren't observed, and it wasn't unusual to hear a store clerk wearily ask a customer, "What do you want now?" Such was the nature of a small island that everyone treated everyone else like family — albeit not a Walton-type family.

Next we scooted off to the post office, where I met Michelle, the postmistress. The post office was in a quaint little building — very ungovernment-like — beside Michelle's tidy-looking farmhouse. Irma told me, and she confirmed this with Michelle, that Michelle and her young family not only heated their home solely with wood but even cooked their meals on a wood stove. How brilliant, I marvelled. In 2001, there were still people — young, educated, and employed — who chose to live by their wits rather than by their wallets.

Our last stop was the airport, where I hugged Irma good-bye. I had chartered a small plane to fly from Windsor to airlift me off the island and fly back to Windsor, where Ted was to pick me up and then drive me back to Hamilton.

The logistics involved in this retreat were insane. So were the costs: in addition to the chartered flight ($160), I had to rent a car ($600) for the three remaining weeks of my urban life.

I was pretty rattled during those final weeks. There were loose ends to tie up at work; the daily commute from Hamilton to Toronto was becoming more intolerable; I erroneously inserted my credit card into an ATM, which promptly ate it; then I ran out of gas on the way home from work one evening — a block, of course, from a gas station. In 30 years of driving, this had never happened to me. It was becoming increasingly difficult for me to find anything endearing about the life I was about to leave. I was chomping at the bit to get out.

To boot, it was Christmas, the most emotionally charged time of the year. In addition to the shopping, the parties, the decorations, and the forced bonhomie, my little family was

47

sullen: this would be our last Christmas in Hamilton. Our cosy Victorian cottage would be put up for sale as soon as Zoë and I left for Pelee Island.

On January 7, Zoë and I loaded our belongings into Ted's Toyota Tercel. The size of his car pretty much dictated what we could take. I resisted the urge to glance back, and we took off on the three-hour drive to Leamington.

I had never actually stopped in Leamington before; I had only driven through it on my way to catch the ferry. Leamington, a typical Ontario small town, enjoys the distinction of being the Tomato Capital of Canada: its main employer is Heinz, the king of ketchup. We were able to see quite a bit of Leamington that day as we drove around in circles looking for the airport. We asked for directions at several gas stations, but shocked attendants professed they didn't know their town even had an airport. During our second — or was it third? — go-round of Leamington, we finally spied an air sock in the distance and drove toward it.

On the runway, we unloaded our provisions, packed in beaten boxes, small, torn suitcases, and even plastic grocery bags. I surveyed this ragtag assortment and wondered why, during all my fevered preparations for this trip, it had never occurred to me to buy real luggage.

As we waited for our departure, my mind swirled with a thousand thoughts. Had I done the right thing? Was it egocentric to follow one's heart? Would this be a positive experience for Zoë? Had I turned off the stove at home?

I sat down on a cement curb beside Zoë and pondered our fate as Ted bounced around with his camera. As a photographer with *The Windsor Star* and, by extension, the *National Post* (since both papers are owned by the same company), he decided to take pictures of me and Zoë. Ted always takes pictures of me when I have no makeup on, my hair is being whipped around by the wind, and the cold air has turned my nose a bright red. I was hoping it was one of those days when he had forgotten to put film in the camera.

"We're ready to go now," a voice announced.

I looked up and saw the pilot walking toward me. He offered to load our nondesigner luggage. Zoë squealed with excitement. She had kept a diary of our trip from Hamilton to Leamington and had made hourly entries. I wondered what was going through her head, but I was too scared to ask her.

Second thoughts were plastered all over my face as Ted walked us to the plane, an eight-seater Caravan. He promised to fly out and visit us in a few days to make sure we were settled.

Within minutes, we were in the air, and I turned to watch the Ontario mainland fade into the distance. I smiled gamely at Zoë. The flight, of course, was a lot shorter than the ferry ride. From Leamington, it took us eight minutes to fly to Pelee Island, enough time for a Heritage Minute and a cup of coffee — though neither was offered. We were barely in the air when it was time to land.

We touched down at Pelee Island International Airport. Zoë and I gave each other thumbs up, and, in the bizarre lingo of the airline industry, we "deplaned." Although the flight had been brief, I felt I was a million kilometres away from anything and anyone I knew.

If you think the airports in the Caribbean are rustic — not much more than thatched-roof huts with a turnstile and a customs officer to stamp your passport — well, Pelee's airport is even more basic. The small, dingy, single-storey, concrete-block building houses a ticket wicket, two washrooms, and 16 rickety seats. Additional seating — it looked like seats pulled from an old hockey arena — are propped against the outside wall of the terminal. The runway stretches west through a field and ends just short of the perimeter road that separates land from lake.

With suitcases and bags in hand, Zoë and I stood like lost orphans on the flat, windswept terrain. I could feel the culture shock setting in as we waited for our ride to arrive. I peered around and saw a man trudging through the snow toward us with a smile on his face.

"You must be Jane. I'm Jim," he said. "And you must be Zoë!"

I was a bit nervous about this meeting. Having worked in the newspaper industry for a long time, I was well aware of Jim's reputation. Jim was a University of Windsor law professor and the outspoken scourge of newspaper owners across Canada. Senior editors and managers returning from journalism conferences would regale the troops with horror stories about the infamous Jim and how he challenged newspaper proprietors on their labour practices. So when Irma had told me Jim would be picking us up, my first thought had been "Oh, great." I knew he lived on the island, but I had been hoping our meeting would be infinitely delayed. Ted, on the other hand, had found the irony delicious and wished he could witness our meeting in person: the handmaiden of the neocon revolution being greeted by a Bolshevik.

Jim and I shook hands, and I thanked him for picking us up. I hoped to God he didn't bring up the *Post*.

"I was really surprised to hear you were coming out here," he said as we settled into his van and began the drive to our island digs. "I didn't think this was the sort of thing the *Post* did."

Gulp. Here it comes, I thought, tensing up. I assured him the *Post* sent its journalists on all sorts of strange and wonderful assignments, though, admittedly, this was one of the strangest. However, I added with an air of authority, the paper was dedicated to exploring different regions of the country, as befits a truly national newspaper. I wasn't sure whether that was crap or not, but it sounded like something a good company person would say. After all, I was now the correspondent for the Pelee Island bureau of the *National Post*. I had an image to maintain and an employer's banner to wave.

Naturally, I wasn't about to tell Jim this, especially since he was at the steering wheel. He delivered us to Irma's house.

I was glad to see that my car, waiting for us in the driveway, had survived the past several weeks without me. After Jim checked the place out for us, made sure the furnace was running, and gave us his phone number in case we ran into trouble, he left.

Zoë and I jumped all over the place, gave each other high fives, and ran up to claim our bedrooms.

I had packed a bottle of wine to celebrate our arrival, and I brought it out. I almost had a stroke when I realized I had forgotten to pack a corkscrew, but eventually I dug out the cork with a knife. I poured Zoë a glass, and we toasted the start of our adventure. And what an adventure it would be.

Chapter 4

WE ARRIVE . . . WITHOUT MILK

*We can see how dangerous individualism can be:
it makes us vulnerable.*
— *General Mandible in* Antz

On our first morning on Pelee Island, I woke up at 7:30 feeling about as in touch with life as Rip van Winkle. However, there was an excitement to waking up in an unknown bed, in an unknown house, in an unknown community, heightened by the knowledge that the unknown often holds surprises. And who doesn't like surprises? Armed with such naïve enthusiasm, I bounded into action that Monday morning.

By 7:30 in my urban life, I had showered, dressed, applied makeup, made the children's school lunches, planned the evening's dinner and simultaneously made breakfast, checked homework, signed school notes, and thrown in a load of laundry. Sometimes I cradled a phone while I did all this, rescheduling appointments and barking orders to anyone and everyone.

By contrast, at 7:30 on my first morning on Pelee, I stood dazed, as if I had a best-before date stamped on my forehead, and it had expired long ago. I quickly scanned my brain's wealth of life skills — skills that, sadly, I knew but hadn't always applied to my life — and dredged up handy Rule 1: Act like you know what you're doing.

I cheerfully woke up Zoë, told her to get ready for school, then headed into the bathroom, closed the door, and wondered whether I had sounded convincingly confident. I ran a brush through my hair, applied lipstick, and then pulled on a pair of jeans and a sweater, in accordance with Rule 2: Look like you know what you're doing. (Lipstick, I've always maintained, is an excellent start. It gives you enough gloss to fool people into believing you've had time to attend to life's details.)

My composure didn't alter when I opened the fridge and saw the scant offerings. "No orange juice today, Zoë, and no milk," I said. "So how about tea and some hot-cross buns?" I made a mental note to pick up some groceries that morning. I hadn't packed juice boxes, so, for the first time in Zoë's school career, the poor kid had to leave the house without one in her lunch bag. "I'll bet you can get a drink from the water fountain at school," I suggested.

Zoë is an intelligent, well-read girl — wise beyond her years — and is passionate about nature and animals. Like most girls her age, she is horse crazy. She loves adventures, and as I watched her eat her breakfast I was overcome with pride at how she had developed into such a lovely, and prepossessed child. This time away will be great for us, I thought. I can really devote my time to her. She, along with her brothers, had shouldered more responsibility than most kids her age, a common reality for children in single-parent families. That responsibility had bred independence, and long ago Zoë had stopped taking advice from me regarding clothing and hairstyles.

But now, with time on my hands, I zeroed in on the mop of hair that obscured her pretty face. "Please go upstairs and brush your hair," I asked. "And put on a hair band."

She stopped in her tracks and gave me that "Excuse me?" look.

I restated my request.

She balked.

I insisted.

Still, she balked.

I threatened to spank her for being disobedient.

She stared at me, then marched upstairs and returned wearing a hair band. She looked beautiful, and I told her so.

Our next little contretemps occurred in the driveway. It had been a few weeks since I had used my car, and I had a momentary lapse about how to work the automatic door locks. With impatience and disgust, Zoë shouted, "Push the top buttons! Duh!!!"

It worked, we got into the car, and I turned to face her. "Don't *ever* speak to me that way again," I said firmly but patiently.

"I was just trying to help," she protested.

"And I appreciate your help but not your tone," I said.

Like every other child on the continent, Zoë was accustomed to delivering a quick, snarky retort — the lingua franca of tweens and teens. It always bothered me when my children used that tone with me, but it was an uphill battle. I figured it would run its course, like pacifiers and Ninja Turtles. It didn't. I should have stopped it when it first reared its head, but, by the time I had decided to deal with it, it had become ingrained in their personalities.

It's always easier for stressed-out, frazzled parents to give in than to face a pint-sized verbal onslaught of "How come? Everyone else does it/has it!" As common courtesies and standards slide on the home front, parents not only become accomplices in their children's poor behaviour but also often adopt it. In the sarcasm department, I was equally guilty.

Now, as the car was warming up, I asked Zoë to join me in pledging that we would use our time on Pelee to change some bad habits. With that, I put the car in reverse, backed out of the driveway, and headed off to the school.

Although I knew the school was at the north end of the island, I was a bit fuzzy on how to get there. Out of the corner of my eye, I could see Zoë biting back the urge to admonish me for my poor navigational skills. By the time we got to the school, I was surprised she wasn't hemorrhaging from biting her lip so much. I had called the school while planning our retreat — a fact I pointed out to Zoë to let her know I wasn't a total moron — and when we arrived the teachers said they were expecting us (I smugly nudged Zoë to indicate I had done my homework, but by now she had tired of the game and gave me that "whatever" look).

Pelee Island Public School, or PIPS as it is affectionately known, is a classic little red schoolhouse built in the 1930s. There had been four schools on the island at the start of the 20th century and nearly 300 school-aged children to fill them. Now there was only one school — kindergarten to grade eight under one roof — and only 30 students. The size of the school may have been an urban parent's dream, but it was an alarming statistic on Pelee Island, underscoring the steady decline of the island's population, especially among its younger ranks.

The three teachers who greeted Zoë and me appeared happy, friendly, and overworked. The spartan conditions were a little surprising, but then I'm not one of those parents who bases the quality of a school on the number of computers in its classrooms. I imagined the eyeball rolling that went on in this school when teachers heard their urban counterparts complain about dwindling preparation times and increasing administrative duties. On the few mornings I called the school to report Zoë's absence, at least one of the teachers was there by 7:15 doing prep work.

The Pelee Project

Zoë's teacher, Mr. Galloway, taught grades three to five in one room. When we walked into his classroom, he introduced us to his students — all seven of them. One was away — "Still in Austria, but she should be back soon," chirped one spunky little blonde girl, who informed us in the same breath that she was leaving for Brazil in a few days to accompany her father, who was in the wine business. Austria? Brazil? So much for my preconceived ideas that island children were shielded from the wider world.

I hugged Zoë good-bye, left the school, climbed into my car, and headed . . . where? I had no job to go to, no appointments to keep.

Normally, I am a fastidiously organized person (or I play at being one in my urban life). I carry a Day-Timer with me at all times: errands, appointments, due dates of bills, to-do lists, and shopping lists are all duly entered. But there on Pelee Island, my Day-Timer was as incongruous as a blood donor clinic at a Kingdom Hall. I felt rather giddy about it: here I was in a car, on an island, with no Day-Timer open by my side.

The white sky, the frozen water of Lake Erie, and the snow-covered ground of the island — air, water, and land — hypnotically blended into one. Big, fat snowflakes began to fall. I felt as if I was seeing the world through fresh eyes, and in a way I was: Pelee's winter landscape was very different from its summer one. Lush foliage had been replaced by brittle and spindly branches; deep snow obscured the boulders that formed the breakwater around the island; cottages that mere months before had teemed with vacationing families were now tightly boarded up. There was no sign of life around except for me and my car.

As I scooted along Pelee's west coast, even my car seemed friskier. I knew I was deluding myself thinking my car had feelings, but at that moment it had the energy of a Labrador retriever pup. Perhaps having been idle for nearly a month, its tires frozen to the Pelee snow, the car was merely having one of those magical automotive moments when mysterious fluids course through valves and a labyrinth of hose. But romantic that I am, I wanted to think that my trusty old Accord felt liberated from urban life too. No more congested highways and pedestrians with death wishes. What's more, it shook off the hang-dog attitude it adopted whenever its nose was forced to sniff the bumper of the car in front of it. On these Pelee roads, it was as if the leash had slipped off its neck.

Thus it was, under such optimistic conditions, that the bottom was destined to drop out: God forbid you should live worry-free, even for a morning, even during a spiritual retreat. As I watched the snow fall, I was jolted out of my reverie by the knowledge that I did have a mission that day: I had to get milk.

I drove to the A.M. McCormick grocery store, but it was closed for the day. I passed the liquor store and would have gone in, but it, too, was closed. I remembered there was a Co-op at the other end of the island, so I turned my car around and made tracks.

The Co-op's grocery supplies were slim, not that I was expecting much from a store that basically sold hardware and farm equipment. I was directed to a tiny room off to one side and found the produce. It wasn't lined up in neat rows like the produce in urban grocery stores, nor did it have a surreal gloss to it. Instead, fruits and vegetables sat in their original packing crates. And the pickings weren't optimum: there was a lone tomato that looked marginally better than the one I had pitched into the compost pile that morning. I humbly added it to my basket. I looked long and hard at a head of iceberg lettuce in an advanced state of limpness, hoping my gaze would transform it into a perky California mix just like they sell at. . . . But I stopped myself. "Buck up, girl," I told myself. "You're on an island now, and iceberg lettuce it is." The radishes looked hardy, so I grabbed a package.

Suddenly, I remembered the milk. As I pulled a bag from the fridge, Sandy, the Co-op's clerk, informed me that milk and bread had to be pre-ordered, and all the bags in the fridge were spoken for.

I placed my order. "When can I pick it up?" I asked eagerly.

"Probably Monday, if the plane arrives," she smiled wanly.

A week without milk? Yikes!

I left the store, and that's when I began to unravel. I spotted a gas pump and decided to fill up my tank. I fumbled with the nozzle and couldn't figure out how to engage the pump. My nose began stinging, the way noses do as a subtle warning that tears are being served up next on the emotional menu.

I felt like a total rube. In fact, I felt like a rube from another planet. The simple things I had done routinely and taken for granted in the city now appeared strange and foreign to me. I couldn't even pump my own gas.

I looked toward the Co-op's window. A gaggle of customers inside the store were watching me, and the moment I looked up they averted their gaze and pretended to be otherwise occupied. I, too, looked away. I was a sideshow: "Watch city woman try to pump gas — and fail!" I had the uneasy feeling that bets were being placed among the locals as to how long I would last. After my little performance at the gas pump, I envisioned a deluge of five-dollar bills hurriedly being thrown down to up the ante.

I paid for the gas (I still remembered how to do that), got into my car, and tried vainly to suppress the tears.

Coming to Pelee Island had involved a number of risks, all of which I had taken in stride. But now the whole exercise inexplicably scared the bejesus out of me, and I wanted to go home.

I admonished myself for not having planned this retreat better. I should have paid attention to our food supply, but back in the city the thought hadn't even crossed my mind. "Bad mother!" I scolded myself. "You think you're so smart in the city, don't you? But you know dick-all out here, sweetheart."

Dick Holl! That's it! I'll go see Dick, the genial bear of a guy who runs the Trading Post! But then I remembered Dick wasn't open on Mondays.

I unfolded the map of Pelee Island that Sandy at the Co-op had given to me. I hadn't thought I would need a map. Sandy had suggested that Just Ask, the island's convenience store (convenient for those who knew where it was), might have milk. I drove along the snowy rural road, the same road, incidentally, that I had driven down after getting off the ferry with my car only weeks before. The mood I had felt then was a sharp and painful contrast to the one I felt now.

Isn't it interesting how your brain automatically defaults to the negative when things don't turn out the way you planned? Can you imagine if people treated failure as a positive experience by saying something like "I blew it! Wow, that's spectacular! I'm so excited about what I've learned from this. Now I'm going to dig myself out of it!" Yes, there probably are people like that in our world, but thankfully they've been dispatched to the Asylum for the Criminally Cheery, where they are enrolled in therapeutic workshops such as How to Lower Your Self-Esteem and Self-Flagellation 101.

By its very definition, risk means the distinct possibility of danger or loss. Even though we put ourselves in risky situations every day — we jaywalk, we drive over the speed limit, we wear chartreuse — we obsess only over our failures, not our successes. Risk, I tried to tell myself, is a necessary ingredient for personal growth. You can't evolve unless you make periodic and temporary escapes from security. If you stick to your comfort zone, you limit your capacity not only to accept change but also to effect change in yourself and in the wider world. You are about as useful to the planet as a rusty nail.

Advertising and the mass media have largely eliminated risk from our lives by instilling in us an exaggerated fear of failure or of being ridiculed by our peers if we take the road less travelled. Instead, we experience risk vicariously through TV game shows and so-called reality programs such as *Survivor* and

Big Brother. We watch people win or lose spectacularly, and their failures — it's always their failures — are the stuff of water cooler conversations the next day.

Before I left on my Pelee Island adventure, friends and colleagues remarked at how "brave" I was to do this. Brave? What did bravery have to do with it? But now, at the moment of meltdown, as I sat in my car on a frozen, lonely island, I understood: "brave" was simply millennium-speak for "unconventional," "freakin' crazy," and "Don't look now, but your career just committed suicide." Was I so hungry for a dose of pure enchantment in my life that I had just seized an opportunity without thinking it through?

I was so involved in beating myself up that I almost missed Just Ask. There wasn't a sign out front or any indication that a store even existed. It looked like an ordinary house. By a clever process of elimination based on the map in my hand — it was the only house in the area — I deduced this must be the place. I entered the driveway, drove around the back, and saw an OPEN sign on a back door.

When I entered Just Ask, I found myself in what amounted to a keeping room — about 15 feet by 15 feet. Its shelves were stocked full of cans and jars and boxes; it was like walking into someone's pantry. For a bizarre moment, the recognition of so many popular brands sent me into an orgasmic orbit. Finally, something looked familiar enough to me that I was reasonably sure I was still on planet Earth. "Oh, there's Dole pineapple chunks! Oh, there's No Name pasta sauce! And could that be? Yes! Yes! Lantic sugar!"

Thankfully, no one was around to witness my insane excitement. I heaped stuff onto the counter and hollered "Hello?" several times. The door connecting the store to the main house eventually opened, and out came a jovial young woman with long, dark hair who introduced herself as Sue.

Sue, it turned out, owned the store with her sister, Connie, headed the island's PTA, and put out Pelee's twice-monthly newspaper, the *Grapevine*. Perhaps it was the dazed look on my face that prompted her to tell me she wasn't a born-and-bred islander. She confided that Pelee had been a bit intimidating to her when she first arrived on its shores several years ago, and it had taken her a while to get used to the place.

Sue had just tallied my bill when I remembered the milk. "That's mine, I'm afraid," she said, wincing when she saw me reaching into the store's fridge. "You have to order in advance. Are you low?"

I told her my tale of woe, and she generously offered me one of her bags.

As I prepared to leave the store, I glanced at the community notice board that hung by the door, and my eye landed on the business card of the island's septic service. Its slogan was "When you're full of shit, call Steingart." This definitely wasn't the mainland.

I drove back to the house, feeling a bit better for having met Sue and having scored some milk. The incident taught me that I couldn't wing it: I needed at least a nominal plan or routine.

After unpacking my groceries, I drew out a sheet of paper and poised my pen. I thought back to my urban life and the habits and routines missing from my rural one. It was like trying to re-create my existence. I glanced around. It was awfully quiet in Irma's house.

Back in my urban life, I constantly had CBC Radio on (well, when I didn't have Madonna or AC/DC in my tape deck), and I discovered, to my horror, that it had been days since the voice of radio host Tom Allen had coaxed me awake. I glanced at the clock. It was almost time for *Disc Drive* with Jurgen Goethe. I plugged in my radio and started fiddling with the dial. I was finally able to locate CBC Radio, though I had to dance around the living room with the antenna for a while until I found clear reception. Once I made contact, the program's familiar theme song was a balm: it was like drinking water after crawling through the desert. Familiarity, in this case, bred contentment.

Dialling into CBC Radio is like setting your emotional compass to "Canadian." I am one of the rare, though I hope not dwindling, breed who listens to CBC 2, its classical station. I know I would be more culturally and socially informed — and, by extension, a better dinner guest — if I listened to CBC 1, but most talk stations are too distracting for me. I find that a steady diet of Mozart and Puccini helps to calm me down. And for the purposes of a spiritual retreat, such a companion is ideal. Now that I had the music and the dulcet voice of Jurgen Goethe — he's like Johnny Carson wrapped in a Hudson's Bay blanket — the edge of my isolation was less sharp.

Zoë would be arriving home soon on a school bus. I was momentarily seized by an urban panic. Would she know where to get off? Whom would I call if she wasn't on the bus? I walked outside and waited by the side of the road, craning my neck to see if the bus was in the distance.

Such worries, I discovered, were unnecessary. The bus stopped in front of our house, and Zoë jumped off. I introduced myself to Deb, the driver. She was, she said, the afternoon driver; her husband, Grant, did the morning run. The bus schedule was easy, she assured me. All I had to do was make sure Zoë was waiting at the roadside by 8:30 a.m. Even I could remember that.

I considered the school bus a total luxury. It wouldn't have been a problem to drive Zoë to school each morning, but it was nice not to have to do it, especially in the winter.

That evening Ted called to see how our first day had gone. I felt silly recounting my search for milk. After more than a year of regaling him with news about my job, the latest office intrigue, my commute, and what the children were squabbling about, I was now giving him a rip-snorting, blow-by-blow account of my search for milk.

However, I could still talk to Ted about the office because I continued to straddle my urban and rural lives. In the first few days of my retreat, there were frantic calls from co-workers with all sorts of pressing questions. Where did I keep the file on such-and-such? Did I have so-and-so's phone number? Who was the contact for this-and-that? As I held the phone to my ear and heard the urgent, breathless requests from my office colleagues, I stared out the window of Irma's house at a landscape that clashed with the world from which these conversations originated. Was there a time when I actually cared about this stuff? My mind had emptied all those petty details, and now I was forced to find them again, pretending to show my colleagues that I was organized, knowledgeable, controlled, perfect, accommodating, and always, *always*, nice.

Likewise, on my urban home front, the alarm system had gone off, prompting worried calls from Paul, the conscientious real estate agent who had listed my Hamilton home. I couldn't totally disconnect from my urban life — not yet.

While Ted's arrival on the island on Wednesday gave Zoë and me the comfort of a familiar face, I was relieved when he left a few days later. Between trying to get my new life in order, sorting out the small fires at work, and running around cooking and tidying up after him, I felt as run off my feet as I was before I got to Pelee.

When Ted phoned later that evening to report that he had arrived safely back in Windsor, I told him I didn't want him visiting us too often. It was hard for me to articulate this without sounding rude, but I wanted him to take my retreat seriously and to respect my privacy. I told him it was a bit difficult conducting a spiritual retreat while someone was stretched out on the sofa in front of me with the crossword puzzle asking, "What's a six-letter word for mollusc?" While Ted was visiting, I had reverted to my well-worn habit of looking after and entertaining those who came to visit me. His visit had resurrected the very habits and routines I was hoping to extinguish.

Ted didn't take my comments very well. I could tell by his voice over the phone that I had taken a chip out of his ego. Still, I was determined not to backpedal. This was my one and only chance to balance my life, and I didn't want to blow it. It was, I also reminded him, the one-year anniversary of my car accident, and I was trying to fulfil a promise to put my life back on track. Ted said he understood, and to let him know when I wanted him back, which was simply man-speak for "Screw you, I won't come out for another month." It was the beginning of a period of tension between us: his need for companionship collided with my need for solitude.

By the end of week one, I was a walking mass of conflicting emotions and sagging confidence. I tried to establish a routine by writing down the days of the week and assigning activities or chores to them, but it was a pointless exercise since I had nothing to do and no way of getting into the island groove. There was a community scattered around me, and I had to find its rhythm and fit in. But without a contact person on the island, I had no one to call and ask "When is the grocery store open? Where do I find a newspaper? What do I do with my garbage? Is there a spa around here?" As much as I craved solitude, it became apparent that, even after warning Ted to stay clear, I needed people around me in order to survive.

Meanwhile, Zoë and I struggled to adjust to our physical surroundings. Nighttime brought an acute awareness that we were, indeed, in a different land. By day, the island was calm and unpretentious. But as afternoon turned quickly into evening — and I don't think I had ever seen a place go from day to night so fast — the blackness was oppressive, smothering, and frightening. There were no streetlights to illuminate the landscape and no carlights. When a car did pass our house in the dead of night, I immediately had visions of the events described in Truman Capote's *In Cold Blood*. As I lay in my bed, it was so dark I honestly couldn't tell whether my eyes were open or shut.

Not that I could sleep. When I wasn't tuned in to my swirling, chaotic internal dialogue, I was tormented by the howling wind that battered my bedroom window and shook the house. I burrowed into my pillow and then tried to wrap it around my head, but the howling intensified. I got out of bed and stumbled around looking for a hooded sweatshirt that would muffle the sound of the wind and warm me up. I was freezing.

This wasn't going to be easy.

Chapter 5

GUILT TRIPS IN TIGHT GENES

*Work? As in honest toil, you mean? Well, I've known a few people
who worked, absolutely swear by it, some of them.*
— *Bertie Wooster*

People equate simplicity with ease. But the reality is that
simplicity isn't easy or natural. As I acclimatized to Pelee life, I
tried to relax and slow down. It was hopeless. Without a to-do
list or a million balls to juggle, I was frustrated and anxious. I

also felt guilty about not having a real job to go to each day. It didn't feel like I belonged to the human race.

It was useless to try to garner sympathy on the matter from anyone on the island because, first, I didn't know anyone, and, second, I couldn't imagine they would comprehend the type of withdrawal I was experiencing. I would just sound like a freak. Slowing down really was like trying to tame a drug addiction.

One of my major struggles was not having places to spend my money — limited as it was. Here I was, barely two weeks into my retreat, and I was dying to shop. I remembered having been inside a tiny gift shop attached to the island's grocery store. I had seen a teapot in there during the summer, and now I wondered whether it was still for sale.

I quickly mastered the grocery store's schedule (though I couldn't, for the life of me, ever figure out which day I was supposed to order milk), and, like the robotic urbanite I was, I drove there almost every day it was open, if for no other reason than to look around. Decades of ritual shopping had forged within me a primal bond with merchandise.

On one such foray that second week, I was at the checkout and nonchalantly asked Kim, the owner of the grocery store, when the gift shop would open.

"It's closed until the spring," she told me while tallying my groceries. Seeing my downcast look — well, maybe it was more like a pout — she asked if there was something I was looking for.

"Yes," I said sheepishly, telling her about the teapot.

Kim pulled out a set of keys from a drawer by the till, walked over to the shop door, and opened it up. "Help yourself," she said as she walked back to the checkout counter.

Wow, a whole store to look in! I didn't know where to begin. I was dying to linger there and admire and fondle all its wonderful wares, but I didn't want to abuse Kim's kindness or make it look like I was a recovering shopaholic. I spied the teapot — it was in the shape of a lighthouse — and decided to buy it. I did need a teapot anyway — well, sort of — and the lighthouse was a bit of a talisman for me. And since it had sat there all these months, and no one had bought it, wasn't it destined to be in my hands? Plus, its price had been reduced. My old acquisitive habits were resurfacing. I had to stop this. I did buy the teapot, but I promised myself to henceforth keep my purchases in check.

Back at my island digs, I carefully unwrapped the teapot, washed it, and gave it a place of prominence on the kitchen counter. I stood back and admired it, pleased with this little purchase.

Then I paced the house restlessly in search of meaningful work. I checked and double-checked my Day-Timer to make sure I hadn't overlooked something — surely there was some crisis I needed to solve or an appointment to keep? But, nope, each blank calendar entry stared back at me with anticipation, hoping I would assign to it some purpose in life. Except for vacations, I had never seen an empty Day-Timer page.

I sat down, and my fingers started tapping the table impatiently. I thought about calling some friends or colleagues, but I was afraid of confessing to them that I was bored out of my skull.

Pause.

I regretted not having sprung for a few of those packaged needlework projects I had seen in a shop in Oakville before I left for Pelee. I could have stitched a set of seat covers by now.

Pause.

It was so quiet I swear I could hear the battery humming in my watch.

Pause.

Boy, I wished I had learned how to knit. The clicking of knitting needles would at least have given the place an air of productivity.

Pause.

I looked at my watch and wondered whether 10:13 was too early to start drinking.

I had, for the first time in as long as I could remember, nothing to do. Nothing. No laundry, no housecleaning, no errands, no screaming kids to threaten. Nothing.

This *was* like curbing an addiction, and I had the symptoms to prove it. My shoulders and neck were tense, and I had periodic spasms inside my skull that, in my newfound paranoia, made me wonder whether the combination of destressing and managing my pent-up restlessness was going to give me a stroke.

I was cursed with a hyperactive mind. Without something to show for my day, I was climbing the walls — not literally, mind you, though the thought did cross my mind. I was that desperate for some form of activity.

The phrase "earning a living" flashed into my brain several times that day, and I realized what an oxymoron it was. What passes as the current pace of work is not about earning a living; it's about earning a death. It's no surprise that the need to work or at least to look busy is strongest in large urban centres, where people work insanely hard and for long stretches at a time. It is a badge of honour to boast that you put in 16-hour days at the office. Such a compulsive attitude has massive repercussions on our health, and it sends to our children the message that work is everything. Must work hard. Even though I knew this, it was hard to break away from thinking otherwise.

I was a miserable failure at trying to detach myself from the workplace teat. I regularly checked my e-mail to keep abreast of the office gossip, sighing over the note that announced the newsroom's Friday-afternoon tradition of cocktail hour.

So my pacing continued. It was like being under house arrest.

In the evening, when I went to bed, I stared at the ceiling and listened to my heart hammer and my head fill with the kind of white noise you hear when you hold a conch shell to your ear. Maybe it was simply blood coursing through my brain, but it was distracting enough to make me wonder whether it was more a symptom of leftover urban angst than normal cerebral activity.

In the morning, I was occupied with getting Zoë ready for school and making her lunch. When she left for school, I was envious. I thought about fabricating an excuse so she could stay home with me, but I couldn't muster the nerve to ask her and appear so pathetically needy.

By the time Zoë returned home from school, I was practically euphoric at having someone to talk to. I listened to her tell me all about her day with such rapt attention that it alarmed her: "Mom, you're scaring me. Why are you so interested in what I did?"

Irma had asked me to water her plants while she was away. I had always been hopeless with houseplants; none of them had ever lasted more than a week. I hoped she wasn't too attached to hers, because they would surely die under my care. Nonetheless, I watered them all and added a note in my Day-Timer to water them each Monday. This was close enough to gainful employment, and I was grateful to have such a menial task to do.

I tried to sit down and read, but the guilt, oh, the guilt! After-dinner reading wasn't a problem, but reading for pleasure during the day? Weren't there bylaws about that sort of thing? I was up against 40-plus years of Protestant work ethic and ill prepared to fight it. I tried to summon my inner couch potato, but I doubted whether a global positioning system could locate it. Relaxing was freaking me out.

The sofa in Irma's living room was located in front of a large picture window facing one of Pelee's main east-west roads. The road was called, not surprisingly, East West Road. Several people rubbernecked as they drove by and actually waved when they saw me sitting in the living room. It was like living in a fishbowl.

I moved away from the picture window and wandered through the house looking for something to do. In front of the small bathroom mirror, I examined the grey hairs multiplying with the speed of flesh-eating disease through my dark locks. It was time for a dye job, but there was no place to buy hair colour on Pelee. No hair salon either. After dealing with my hair, I began scrutinizing my face and had a lively and highly edifying debate with myself over whether I needed cosmetic surgery. We (myself and I) decided to defer the decision but promised to watch for signs of further facial deterioration. Fortunately, the lack of a full-length mirror in the house prevented a more intensive discussion on the subject.

During my perusal of Irma's bookshelves, I found a number of New Age-type books. There were books on everything from intuitive touch to cranial-sacral therapy — in short, not the type of material you would find on the average senior citizen's bookshelves. I was pretty impressed. I pulled out several books, including *The Prophet*, and added them to my reading list. I figured that if I made reading *look* like work then I could convince myself that it *was* work — it was research.

Just when I started to believe I was the only one stupid enough to actually attempt life off the beaten track — everyone seemed to be talking about it, but who actually did it? — I flicked on the TV. One of the afternoon programs had a story about a lawyer who had been assigned to a high-profile case. The woman was obviously excellent at her job, but one day she stunned her associates by announcing that she wouldn't take the case after all. To do so would compromise her desire for balance; the workload would wear her down and prevent her from enjoying life. Instead, she informed her colleagues, she was leaving the firm so she could teach yoga. She wanted more from life than the dubious glory that accompanies a meaty legal case. That gave me a boost. I wasn't the only oddball out there;

The Pelee Project

I had company. There were at least two of us.

During the week, I caught wind of an interesting anecdote, and, trying to be the faithful correspondent that I was, I made some calls, crafted a news story, and fired it off to the *Post*.

The story concerned an altercation between one of the islanders and a pilot for the airline that transported islanders to and from the mainland each day. At the time, the transportation contract was awarded to an airline that tacked the Pelee Island run onto its regular Toronto-Windsor-Toronto bank and mail delivery service. The short haul to Pelee was considered a hassle for the pilots, prompting an off-the-cuff comment from one of them that "The best thing that could happen to Pelee Island would be to nuke it."

It was a quirky, provocative little story, and the *Post*'s editors were keen on it — initially. Then they began reworking it to death, trying to turn it into a feature-length story, which it most certainly wasn't. When that didn't work, they returned it to its initial form and analysed it for three days, finally ditching it in favour of another equally innocuous story.

I was past caring, frankly, but because my research had involved calls to people who had successfully avoided media scrutiny in the past — Pelee's reeve, officials at the government-run airline, the islander involved in the spitting match — my little unpublished story ruffled some feathers and cast some suspicion on me. In the city, I could have disappeared into the crowd; on a sparsely populated island, that was pretty much impossible.

Just as I was about to slink back to the sofa and give sloth another chance, the islander involved in the story — Norm —

phoned me and invited me to his house for coffee. Being a cynical journalist, I figured he was trying to butter me up about the story, but nothing could have been further from the truth. Next to last week's map lesson (always carry a map), this was my second revelation: sometimes people don't have ulterior motives. For a journalist, this was a biggie — on par with a child finding out that Santa doesn't fly through the night delivering presents. Journalists are trained to be wary of those who might influence us or make us so comfortable that we lose our edge or our impartiality. But as I learned, people on Pelee didn't give a damn about influencing others. If you didn't subscribe to their point of view, you were simply frozen out socially and exiled to the opposing team.

Norm was one of the first Pelee people I formally met. He was a tall, rugged, middle-aged man with a grey beard and narrow, kind eyes. He greeted me at his front door, and led me through the kitchen and into the family room where his fax machine was spitting out papers. "Some investment advice," he told me. He and his wife, Ann, had a lovely home. As we settled into a getting-to-know-you conversation, I learned they also possessed a charming personal story. Both had grown up on Pelee and dated throughout school. After high school, they had broken up, left the island, gone their separate ways, married other people, endured individual disappointments and sadness, divorced their spouses, bumped into one another years later, rekindled their romance, got married, and moved back to Pelee.

There are probably a million stories like that in the world, but I was nonetheless struck by how we humans go to great lengths to change ourselves and our lives when everything we really need is already within our grasp; we just fail to recognize it. It is human nature to take the long way (and the hard way) when it comes to discovering what we value, but eventually all roads lead home. Sometimes people need to reaffirm their paths by taking detours, just to satisfy themselves that there really is no better route. Hmmm. Sounded familiar.

Coffee with Norm was convivial, and he pulled out homemade chocolate chip cookies and coerced me into trying one. OK, two. I waved good-bye to my journalistic impartiality as it flew out the window.

Norm and I barely talked about the "nuking" incident. Rather, he tried to coach me on Pelee's peculiarities. There were, he told me, a number of cliques on the island, and I should tread cautiously. I thanked him for his kind advice, though I doubted I would need it. I could barely navigate my way around the island, I told him, let alone through the myriad social circles of Pelee Islanders. Norm smiled politely.

I was sorry when our coffee klatch ended. I privately wondered whether Norm and I could adopt a weekly get-together; then I could get to know four more people and have a regular coffee day with each one of them to fill my weekdays. I thought back to my urban life and how I had wished I had taken more people up on their offers to join them for morning coffee at the local Tim Hortons outlet.

Back at Irma's house, Norm's cookies gave me an idea: I had time to bake and cook to my heart's content.

I have a narrow repertoire when it comes to cooking. I don't collect cookbooks; I don't even know which spices go best with certain foods. Once, when I raved about a soup in a rather fancy restaurant, I called over the waiter and asked him to identify the dark, flavourful bits floating in my soup. "That would be basil," he deadpanned and walked away, clearly disgusted that the restaurant had deigned to allow such an ignorant customer into its premises.

I thumbed through the two cookbooks I had brought with me in search of a recipe that was moderately challenging, would guarantee success, and called for easy-to-obtain ingredients. Having found a lone package of raw cranberries — *cranberries*, of all things — at the Co-op, I made cranberry muffins. These elicited a rare compliment from Zoë when she returned home from school, even though the bottoms were burnt.

My culinary feats weren't enough to keep me from checking out the Friday lunches at the Legion, a weekly winter tradition on Pelee Island that Norm had told me about. For five dollars, you received a hot, hearty, home-cooked meal with three salads. This particular week, one of the salads consisted of baby greens, which I guessed had a street value on the island of $50 an ounce. Rumour had it that this stash had been smuggled in from Ohio.

I was just digging into my Legion meal when in walked a party of four led by a short, burly guy. He picked me out of the crowd quickly and swaggered over. I figured he was going to introduce himself, but the look on his face told me otherwise. As he neared me, he bellowed, "I have a bone to pick with you, young lady." I stopped eating, and a nervous silence fell over the

Legion. I figured the fellow was going to take issue with something that had appeared in the *National Post*, an occupational hazard. Newspaper minions are routinely held accountable for editorial decisions and opinions made at least 23 steps above them on the totem pole. I braced for the usual line: "You tell Conrad, next time you see him, that. . . ." But the complaint wasn't directed at the newspaper's proprietor; it was directed at me. "You didn't wave to me," he said loudly, then extended his hand and introduced himself as Ed.

Ohmigod. He was right. The first law of island etiquette was to wave to people you pass on the road. I had been pretty vigilant about this, but I recalled passing someone earlier in the week and, immersed in some great thought, forgetting to wave. I realized this as soon as I had passed the driver, and I hoped he hadn't noticed. But Ed had noticed. And now he was standing in front of me, wagging his chubby finger.

I apologized profusely and made a comment about being a Toronto bitch: the only wave we urban motorists give each other is of the middle-finger variety. That got a laugh, but Ed's rebuke rang with a simple truth: people everywhere want to be noticed and needed. In our urban lives, we work like demons in order to get stroked. We are stripped of our identities, we are reduced to the swipe of a card, and then we adopt a reductionist mode of behaviour. We greet one another with "How's it going?" or "How are you?" But we don't really care to hear the answer. We rush from one person to the other with the same fatuous greeting and receive a similarly vacuous answer: "Great." "Fine." "Can't complain." Well, of course you can't complain —

no one has the time for or the interest in your complaint.

At that moment in the Legion, I wanted to stand up on the table and issue a full public confession of all my fast-living sins. "Please, somebody help me. I just wanna slow down!"

By the end of week two, I had met a few people, but I also felt isolated from my urban connections. It was as if I was in exile, Pelee was my Elba.

The isolation was magnified by a few personal milestones later in the week. It was my son Adam's 17th birthday, and this was the first time I hadn't been there to celebrate it with him. I telephoned Adam, but it wasn't the same, and the sound of his voice made me melancholic and homesick. I thought back 17 years to the day of his birth and was stunned by what had transpired in both our lives. Seventeen years wasn't that long, yet so much of life had passed in the interim.

It was also the second anniversary of the death of my father, and I was still grieving his absence. His death from cancer had been expected, but even in expectation there is denial. Two years later, our family was still reeling from the shock. I wondered what Dad would have thought about this retreat.

To cap off the week, my mother phoned. I could tell from the tightness in her voice that it wasn't going to be an uplifting call. A few weeks earlier, she had been excited by my sabbatical to Pelee Island, but this week — no doubt overcome with memories of my father — I could tell she was regarding me as a deserter. After listing her sundry complaints and minor ailments, she sighed: "But don't worry about me," which, if you are conversant in mom-speak, translates into, "Why the hell aren't you here to look after me?" I felt guilty for not being the daughter she wanted. By this stage of her life, she had hoped that I would have a nice husband and home life, and that I wouldn't need to run off to some godforsaken island to find my soul. Adding to my guilt was the fact that I had to ask her for money to cover some bills.

It was enough to make me want to pack up and return home. But I was making progress. It was only the third time that week that I had wanted to bail out. The week before, I had chalked up eight bail-out moments.

Chapter 6

PELEE PROTOCOL

In social matters, pointless conventions are not merely the bee sting
of etiquette, but the snake bite of moral order.
— Florence King

The milestones from the previous week made me grateful for the
isolation so that I could contemplate them at length and in
peace. Marking personal milestones away from your usual
environment allows you to put some space between the occasion

and the inherent traditions, reactions, and expectations. It prevents milestones from becoming more like millstones.

There was another milestone this week: my birthday. I had given birth to Adam a week before I turned 30, and here I was, 17 years later, examining the distance I had come. I felt sad about the two marriages I had lost. Divorce takes a terrible toll. Much has been written about the effects of marriage break-down on children, but few people have acknowledged the debilitating and lasting effects on adults. Books on the subject seem to want you to just hurry up and vault over the emotional hurdle and carry on with your life — as if that were the only, and most important, aspect. I had weathered two divorces, and it astounded me that I was still able to walk, talk, and blow bubbles at the same time.

I summoned up my girlhood dreams and compared them to my current situation. As a girl of 10 — Zoë's age — I had looked ahead to 2001 and imagined that I would have a stable, happy marriage (only one, thank you), a brood of children (I wanted 10!), a comfortable home, a job, and a sober, relatively calm life. Boy, was I off track. And while I despaired over the life that never was, I felt a strange contentment and an under-standing of why things had to be the way they were.

A recurring dream of mine involved being imprisoned in a darkened castle surrounded by a moat. When I was younger, I figured it simply meant I was doomed to a sad, lonely, and stagnant life as the wife of Prince Charles, a realization I bore rather stoically, I thought. As I got older, I saw that the dark castle was not a castle but an unlit lighthouse, and the dream underscored my sense of feeling different, even slightly isolated, from others. Now I saw that *I* was the darkened lighthouse — my inner light had dimmed — and that the water surrounding me was Lake Erie. It was my duty to restore my light. It was suddenly obvious why I had felt such an instant affinity with Pelee's lighthouse when I first saw it the previous summer. Like me, it was undergoing a renovation after years of neglect.

Maybe my life was on track after all. All my steps (and apparent missteps) had brought me to Pelee Island. Maybe I was meant to be here.

To avoid being branded a delusional old broad, I kept this little revelation to myself. I certainly wasn't about to tell Ted this when I flew to Leamington to meet him this week. I was low on cash, and the absence of banks and banking machines forced me off the island and back into urban life — for a day. After packing Zoë off to school, I drove to the airport and boarded a plane for the mainland.

Ted had the day off, and, though he was still miffed at being banished from the island, he agreed to meet me at Leamington's airport and chauffeur me around on various errands. We had six hours before the plane's scheduled return to Pelee Island.

I had been away from mainland life for only three weeks, but my senses had evidently undergone a decompression of sorts because they were rudely and suddenly jolted by the visual and aural assaults of screaming billboards, road signs, traffic lights, display windows, cars and pedestrians darting out every-where, the smell of exhaust fumes, the abrasive rattle of trucks, the grit from the road kicked up as they barrelled past us, a landscape of logos — and this was just Leamington! How would I readjust to Toronto?

I stopped my hand from raising reflexively whenever a car drove by or when I made eye contact with people. In such a short period of time, my Pelee wave had become as natural a response as breathing.

Ted found this all rather amusing. The woman who had easily navigated the treacherous Toronto streets, and could scan a jeweller's display window from 10 metres while driving past it at 60 kilometres per hour, was now overwhelmed by a small Ontario town.

Our first stop was the drugstore, where I executed a clever magic trick: I walked in with a three-item list and came out with six items in a bag. Next was the grocery store. I nearly convulsed over the sheer quantity of food — baked goods as far as the eye could see, row upon tidy row of cans, cartons, bottles, and jars. I asked Ted to keep me focused and then promptly sent him off on an errand while I drooled over the pastry counter.

My brief time on Pelee had imbued me with a rare sense of patience and friendliness, but it didn't take me long to realize that I still didn't possess a bottomless reserve of those qualities. As I approached the refrigerated bin that held an assortment of small cooked hams, a department manager was furiously straightening out the lot of them so they would be lined up neatly and orderly. I stood by his side waiting for a break in his feverish sorting so I could grab a ham. He didn't budge, even though he was quite aware of my presence. I cleared my throat to signal that I was waiting. Still he ignored me. I reached past Mr. Ham Sorter. I was willing to give him the benefit of the doubt: perhaps he was, indeed, lost in thought and hadn't noticed me standing there after all. Surely he would move aside when he realized he was in my way. Wishful thinking. When I selected a ham, Mr. Ham Sorter glared at me, as if I had the nerve to ruin his neat work. I responded with my well-honed ocular technique of simultaneously widening my eyes and rolling them upward, a gesture that said "I am the paying customer here, and you, sir, are a person who is fetishizing the organization of hams." I walked away in a huff and several paces later turned to transmit a final salvo, but he was hunched over his ham bin, continuing his obsessive work.

Elsewhere in this vast A&P were similar dour-looking men, all appearing as if they had received some stinging rebuke in bed from their wives the night before. Maybe ham sorting was a metaphor.

I gravitated toward the female clerks, who, when they had finished their excruciatingly long conversations about nothing with one another, paused to consider my request for assistance and then signified that it wasn't part of their job descriptions by resuming their conversation.

At the checkout, I requested a box for my groceries. The cashier gave me a blank look that said bags or nothing. I told her it had to be a box since the groceries were being transported on a plane.

"We don't have boxes," she said flatly.

"You must have boxes, you're a major grocery store," I countered.

"Well, maybe *he*," she said, cocking her head toward Ted, "can go find one."

"Where do I go?" asked Ted helpfully, trying to diffuse the onset of an argument.

"Down *there*," she said, now cocking her head in another direction.

When Ted set off, I asked She Who Cocks Her Head, "Couldn't you just pick up your phone and call a department manager or someone in Customer Service to bring a box to us?"

Another dead look as she limply picked up the phone. Honestly, the staff in this store were like extras in *The Invasion of the Body Snatchers*.

Mr. Ham Sorter came rushing onto the scene and looked none too pleased about having been dragged away from his fulfilling vocation to understudy the role of Box Finder. I glanced over at Customer Service and noticed the Three Clerks were raptly listening to their colleague's detailed — painfully detailed, I might add — account of her aunt's operation.

"What a cranky store," I said loudly to Ted as we exited the A&P, the P surely standing for purgatory.

I looked at my watch and let out a groan — we had five more hours in Leamington. Pulling out my list, I directed Ted downtown. Our next mission was to find a cartridge for my computer's printer.

We walked into Bateman's Stationery. Immediately, a store clerk called out (dare I say cheerfully?) "Hello."

Smarting from the A&P experience, I nodded curtly and started browsing.

"Can I help you?" the clerk asked.

I figured the comment was merely code for "I'm busy, so don't ask me to help you even though I've offered to do so." I said, "No, thank you," and made my way toward the printer cartridges.

The clerk then came over and insisted on helping me in my search. I lamely mentioned the cartridge I needed, privately invoking a tired stereotype that, since she was an older woman, she probably was unfamiliar with such things.

"Oh, yes, for an Epson 740," she murmured correctly. "I think we're out of stock on that one." She hurried over to her computer to check the inventory. "Yes, we are out of stock," she confirmed, "but let me call around." She then picked up the phone and did just that. She found what I was looking for — at a competitor's store — and asked that the cartridge be held for me.

I was gob-smacked by this display of genuine customer service. The clerk then led Ted and me through the door and onto the sidewalk and gave us specific instructions on where her competitor was located. It was within walking distance.

At our destination, I purchased the cartridge and imperiously told the young sales clerk who rang it up about the lesson I had just learned about true customer service. "Make sure you return the favour to that woman at Bateman's," I told her. "She gave you business today."

The befuddled young clerk assured me the two stores routinely cooperated, and no doubt she invoked her own tired stereotype that I was a middle-aged pain in the ass.

By now, Ted had exhausted his bottomless well of patience and suggested we go for lunch to celebrate my birthday. He would rather have pins stuck in his eyes than shop.

We settled into a table at Gilligan's, a roadhouse-type establishment that offered exotic burgers: buffalo, ostrich, emu. We received great service, and, when we each asked for a glass of wine, it was served in a glass with a generous bowl, not in those thimble-sized glasses used by most restaurants that make you wonder whether wine has suddenly been rationed. I swear, I get more wine at a communion rail than I do in some restaurants.

After lunch, I found a hair salon, Chez Suzie, that dispensed with the snobbery of making you beg for an appointment and took me as a walk-in customer. Suzie herself attended to me. She was a bright, impossibly gorgeous young woman, as skilled with her scissors as she was at running her business. One hour of her vivacity lifted my spirits so much that I was almost ready to forgive Mr. Ham Sorter. Almost.

It was nearly 4 p.m. and time for Ted to return me to the airport.

The plane was waiting for us when we arrived, and the pilot asked if he could load my groceries onto the plane. Could he? It was one of those moments women live for: a smiling man offering you his help and making you feel like a queen in the process. I had been taken out for lunch, someone had fussed with my hair (is there a dreamier sensation?), and now someone wanted to load my groceries onto a plane. Ahhh, life didn't get much better than. . . .

A voice jerked me back to reality. Ed was moving toward me and looking none too pleased. Oh, God, I thought, he's going to berate me for not having waved to him on the streets of Leamington. I knew I shouldn't have listened to Ted about that waving thing.

"Where have you been?" Ed asked pointedly.

"Hey, I'm four minutes early," I protested.

"Yeah, well we've been waiting 15 minutes. If you had got here earlier, we could have been home by now."

I looked at the pilot, who seemed sheepish. "Sometimes, if all the passengers are here," he explained gently, "we fly out earlier. We don't always stick to the departure time if everyone's ready to go."

I kissed Ted good-bye and boarded the plane.

"What's your rush, Ed?" I asked curiously as we settled into our seats and struggled with our seatbelts. Maybe he had been to the A&P too.

He told me that, although he and his wife, Lee-Ann, had had a nice enough day in Leamington, he had missed the island.

I found this quaint and endearing, especially in a burly fellow like Ed. In fact, I had sensed this among the other passengers on the flight over that morning. Everyone was animated as the plane roared down the runway, but they all suddenly became lost in their own worlds as they stared out the plane's windows at the diminishing view of their island, reluctant to lose sight of it.

The same thing happened on the return flight to Pelee: lots of talk during the flight over the frozen lake, but as soon as the island came into view everyone stopped chatting and craned their necks to put Pelee in their sights. It was like a human version of photosynthesis.

When I arrived home, Zoë was already back from school. I checked our phone messages and found one from an islander named Franny, who, she informed me rather imperiously in the message, had been asked by Irma to take me under her wing. Having just returned from a holiday, Franny was now "bahk on the aahland," her dusky voice announced, and she expected Zoë and me for dinner at Blueberry Hill at five — that day.

I was taken aback for several reasons. First, I had no idea where Blueberry Hill was. Second, it was already 4:30, and I hadn't properly replied. Third, it was a school night, and it was a long-held tradition in my family that no good ever came of going out on a school night. Fourth, I had never been *told* to come for dinner, I had always been *asked*, but this was a clear command. Fifth, I had been taught not to accept sudden invitations, that there was supposed to be a three-day period of grace between the invitation and the actual event.

It dawned on me that I had become so anal retentive about ridiculous rules of protocol that I actually tried to talk myself out of accepting a gracious invitation to dinner. How had I become so rigid about such things? Where had I learned these lessons? Sometimes we impose the most ridiculous restrictions on ourselves, and over time they become learned behaviours. Then we wonder why there's no fun in life. If I hadn't come to Pelee, how long — if ever — would it have taken me to see how firmly my sphincter was clenched?

I felt giddy as I told Zoë we had been invited out for dinner — that night.

She studied me gravely. "But, Mom, it's a school night. What are we going to do?"

"We're going to go," I said, a smile creeping over my face. It was worth it just to see the look on Zoë's face as an old rule disintegrated before her eyes. She let out a whoop of delight. "Oh, Mommy, I love you," she said.

As I hugged her, I hoped this would be the start of more school-night outings. It would show her that old dogs can and do learn new tricks. And I hoped she, too, would learn to indulge her spontaneous spirit and not let it get tied up in outmoded dictums.

Jim and Gail had also been invited to dinner that night. Since they lived just down the road from us, they offered to drive us to Blueberry Hill.

"What's she like?" I asked, hoping to get the inside scoop on this Franny person. But Jim and Gail only said she was lovely and funny and wild.

And she was. Franny greeted us with all the flair and ease of a true chatelaine as she flung open the door of her beautiful home and stood silhouetted in soft light and candlelight. The table was exquisitely set with gleaming silverware. I nudged Zoë and directed her eyes to the table: real cloth napkins! A bouquet of yellow sweetheart roses was the only contrast to the blueberry-coloured table setting.

The convivial surroundings — and a large glass of wine — settled my initial flutter of nerves. Franny's place was gorgeous, and I decided that I could live there.

Franny and I took an instant liking to one another. She was an elegant, frightfully thin, Bacall-voiced gal with a raucous laugh. She liked her Scotch neat and her cigarettes lit, and she presided over Blueberry Hill with regal authority. She had a colourful past, and she managed to withhold just enough information to make it more so.

Franny and Zoë also hit it off. Zoë has long preferred the company of adults to children, mainly because "adults have way more interesting stories." But in Franny she also found her card-playing match. She was in heaven.

My retreat now three weeks old, I was beginning to get into the Pelee groove. I had figured out the grocery store's schedule (Tuesday, Wednesday, and Thursday 8 a.m. to 2 p..m.; Saturday 8 a.m. to 5 p.m.; closed Sunday, Monday, and Friday); Just Ask's was Monday to Saturday 10 a.m. to 3 p.m.; Wednesday, Friday, and Saturday evenings 6 p.m. to 8 p.m.; Sunday 11 a.m. to 2 p.m. Even the Liquor Control Board of Ontario couldn't be relied on for regular hours (Tuesday to Saturday 9:30 a.m. to 6 p.m., closed Sunday, Monday, and lunch hours, though there was no mention of just when "lunch" was). After a life of 24-hour shopping, I now had to pay attention not just to the day of the week but also to the time of day.

The Pelee Island Trading Post had an easier schedule; it was only open Fridays and Saturdays (or by appointment, as I later discovered), and I had learned from Irma and Franny that the Anglican church services were every second week at 10 a.m. The Co-op had the most regular hours at Monday to Friday 9 a.m. to 3 p.m. If for nothing else, my trusty Day-Timer was handy when it came to recording Pelee's erratic schedules.

Much of my information in this regard was gleaned from the *Grapevine*, Pelee's newspaper, really a sheaf of photocopied 8 x 11 sheets of paper stapled together. It was published every two weeks and was available only at certain outlets — which necessitated another probe of the exact day when it would appear and where it could be obtained.

The *Grapevine* listed the timetables of the island's handful of commercial outlets and posted birthdays and anniversaries, items for sale, equipment or people for hire, the menus of the weekly lunches at the Royal Canadian Legion, the dates of upcoming euchre tournaments, and the meetings of town council. But there was little actual news in it. For instance, while readers were sometimes apprised of upcoming council meetings, these meetings were never covered. I couldn't understand how an island could operate in such a communication vacuum.

This week I attended a council meeting along with Ted, Gail, and Jim. Jim was a professor of media law, Ted was a news photographer, and both Gail and I were journalists. As we watched the proceedings, I figured Pelee Township had never had such a contingent of media hounds in its presence, yet the reeve and the councillors were oblivious to the fact. Some of their comments were a reporter's dream, and after the meeting all four of us swooned at the mileage we could have got out of it for our respective newspapers. Sadly (though perhaps luckily for township councils everywhere), newspapers consider regional and township governments below their dignity to cover. Too bad: they are missing the most entertaining stories.

I got most of my local news by word of mouth. "Did you know the ferry schedule might change?" someone asked me.

"Why, no," I replied. Then I was told of an upcoming transportation meeting, its date, time, and venue to be announced — I had no way of knowing how.

"Did you hear that Lyle's truck went through the ice when he tried to drive to Kelly's Island?" another person asked me. Again I had to plead ignorance and was given the details. Apparently, in very cold winters, it's possible to drive across Lake Erie to the neighbouring U.S. islands, where there are bars and a modicum of nightlife. Pelee's history is generously sprinkled with terrible tragedies involving carloads of families or friends whose vehicles plunged through the ice as they attempted their own passage to the islands or the mainland. Thankfully, nothing tragic had befallen Lyle, except that he was the subject of a few chortles.

Occasionally, I would extract a few nuggets of news at the liquor store, where Al, the island's reeve, was its manager. The hot topic on the island was usually transportation.

Without real news, the *Grapevine*'s personality was forged in its quirky notices. "If anyone found two hammers at Lester's barn on East West Road, it would be great if you could return them to the Co-op. Thank you." "Three big carving knives with LEGION burnt into the plastic handles are missing from the

Legion. Please return as soon as possible. Thank you." "Lost: Black and white cat (mostly black). Very friendly. Has extra digits on paws."

What caused the most commotion, however, were the anonymous submissions from islanders complaining about the lack of community spirit. The following missive appeared that week.

> Wintertime on Pelee, for some, means free time, so why can't we find the time to get involved? The roads to get to places where events are being held aren't very long, but they seem to be not very well travelled. Our houses are pretty close together, but we as neighbours aren't very close. . . . It may be that it's more important to ask who's going to be there before you ask what time you should be there. It may be easier to talk about someone behind their back and believe whatever you've heard to be true, than to talk to the person face to face and believe what they tell you to be true. . . . Why can we say "hi" to our fellow islanders when we see them on the mainland, but we can't sit next to that person for bingo, cards or crafts? Other islands have different activities, such as an island scavenger hunt, where the whole community plays. Pelee could do the same, only it would probably be a hunt to find enough people to play. . . . Would it be better to live in a big city

where no one waves when they pass you in
their car, no one brings your dog back when it
gets loose, and where it costs a lot more for a
night out? . . .

I was stymied. Was it so difficult for people to get along,
even on an island? Surely this was an isolated case. Every
community has its curmudgeon, and perhaps this anonymous
writer was that person, I reasoned. I refused to believe that
Pelee was anything but a perfect oasis in a chaotic, troubled
world. I was so naïve.

Chapter 7

DRY SKIN, DRY SOUL

Years may wrinkle the skin, but to give up enthusiasm wrinkles the soul.
— *Samuel Ullman*

Two weeks earlier, at Zoë's urging, I had decided to get into an exercise routine. I think Zoë was secretly worried that she would return home from school one day and find her mother in front of the TV wearing track pants and stuffing her face with bonbons. But exercise was the perfect antidote for my excess energy. Plus, I needed to do it. I thought I had spent the past 25 years working my ass off, but a backward glance in the mirror that week proved otherwise.

What I quickly settled on was a walk around the block — a seven-kilometre block to be exact. Every morning, after I put Zoë on the bus, I faced the elements and headed off on my walk. This was a good thing, because by week 4 I needed a diversion — and badly.

My retreat was nearly a month old, and I continued to obsess over my appearance. I surprised even myself at the extent of my shallowness. It wasn't so much that I cared how I looked — it was great to be free of makeup and restrictive clothing — but it concerned me that no one cared how I looked. What a marked contrast to the appearances-are-everything way of life in the city, where a hefty portion of your personal cachet is measured through the lens of labels, brands, and affiliations. It was very weird being in a place where none of that mattered.

I mulled this fact over as I headed out on my daily walk. In small communities the world over, visual trappings don't matter the way they do in large cities. Yet millions of people have become so conditioned by the powerful and tempting messages manufactured by big cities that they begin to believe they are the only messages that matter.

As much as I tried to tell myself that I was here to restore my inner self, I couldn't tear myself away from dealing with my external self. So much for "begin within" and trying to fashion a loving heart. I had horrible visions that I would work so hard on relighting my soul and polishing my inner beauty that I would emerge from my retreat looking like a hag. And what would people say then? "Well, look at her. Went off to find her soul, and she returns looking like a 90-year-old. Give me road rage, double lattes, and demanding bosses any day!"

That possibility led to heated debates with myself over whether, given the ways of the world, it was better just to work on my external self and leave it to chance that someone might stumble across my kind-heart-in-progress. After all, you're not likely to hear a wolf whistle followed by the words "Wow, nice soul." My facial lines, greying hair, and thickening waistline would be what people saw. Besides, in such a fast-paced world, no one really gives a hoot about your soul. So why worry about it? For me, the answer was obvious: I was restoring my soul for myself, not for someone else.

Unaccustomed to hearty, daily walks, my citified skin faced more of nature's winter wrath than it had in a long time. After returning to the house after my walk, I decided to do something about the effect of dry weather on my itchy skin. Without a spa around, I cobbled together one in my kitchen with the few items I had on hand. I boiled water on the stove, then used a towel to cover both my head and the simmering pot. The steam washed over my face and opened up the pores. After 10 minutes, I patted my skin dry and applied a mask — one of those small packets you buy at drugstores for 99¢. Then I lay down on the sofa — praying that no one would knock on my door or peek in my window. The sight would have turned anyone to stone. After 20 minutes on the sofa, I gently washed off the mask and applied a heavy moisturizer. I pumiced my feet and scrubbed my hands. After manicuring my nails, I topped them with a pale shade of polish and lathered on a heavy moisturizer.

The whole procedure cost me pennies, not the usual $150 or so at a real spa. I congratulated myself on my newfound thriftiness and resourcefulness.

What I really craved was a good hot soak in a tub, but the iron level in the water was so high on this part of the island that it turned the water dark yellow. It would have been like bathing in a tub of urine. No amount of bubble bath or visualization would have made it seem like anything else.

I began to warm to my simple, limited, and highly unfashionable wardrobe — half a dozen sweaters and about four pairs of pants. It was a huge relief not to be wearing the straitjacket clothing of the business world — or any clothing that didn't have an elastic waistband. I revelled in the physical freedom: I could run, jump, walk fast, walk slow, without my clothing hindering my movements. I had brought a few pairs of thick work socks, the kind men wear with construction boots or hockey skates. I couldn't get enough of them. They were so comfortable.

Wearing dull, serviceable clothing helped me in my quest for serenity. There was nothing sexy or colourful about it — everything I had brought with me was either black or grey. It wasn't attractive, but neither did it feel as if I had donned a hair shirt.

Past experience had taught me that a lack of colour was necessary during periods of transition. When I went through a particularly upsetting divorce and was setting up my new home, I opted for colours that were so neutral and boring they almost induced narcolepsy. I couldn't begin to pick out paint colours because I had no colour in my life. As I gained confidence in being single again, I gradually added colour to my home and to my life — literally and metaphorically.

It was during week 4 that I leafed through *Simplicity* by the modern philosopher Edward de Bono. While he doesn't specifically refer to colour, he notes that, in making sense of things that are complex, you need to disassemble the components, reduce the structure to its core, and start over again. Only from a clean (and colourless) slate can you start to rebuild. Like peeling an onion, this is often impossible to do without tears, but it can also be a rejuvenating and purifying experience. What's raw and tender becomes firmer and resilient once it's exposed. When you come clean, you heal.

In a way, this retreat *was* like a spa. I was undergoing spiritual exfoliation, and the layers that had kept my soul shrouded and buried were being sloughed off.

Naturally, it's always easier to look into a mirror than into your soul, so I peered at my mirror image and tried to exfoliate some self-image problems. Like the majority of women my age, I had gradually gained weight over the past few years, and while I was a little taken aback by it, when I stopped to think I figured I was pretty lucky I hadn't ballooned to elephantine proportions since I never met a sweet I didn't eat or an exercise routine I stuck to.

We obsess over our weight when really, if we're totally

honest with ourselves, we have the bodies we deserve. How long are we going to suck in our tummies before we figure out that there really is no point in doing so? If you eat healthy food regularly, you'll end up with a healthy, regular body. If you starve yourself or feed yourself far less than your body requires, you'll end up with an unnaturally thin body. If you eat more than your body requires, you'll end up with an unnaturally large body. There really is no big mystery to this, though you would never know it if you passed a magazine rack. The promise of magic bullets only feeds our neuroses. But when we let go of this part of ourselves, we release all sorts of suppressed expectations and in turn free our spirits, thereby living more naturally and happily. When we hold on to unreal and unattainable self-images, we're really holding ourselves back from expressing our true personalities. At least that's what I tried to tell myself.

If I was having difficulty letting go of some old habits, I was making progress that week in other areas. I was becoming more social.

By now, I could recognize many islanders on a first-name basis, a major accomplishment since I have always been bad with names — sometimes I even forget my own. But now I made a deliberate effort to learn not just their names but also who they were — who they *really* were. I was entranced by how they had come to live on Pelee Island, what their backgrounds were, where their families hailed from, and what they thought of island life.

One day, as I got out of my car at the Co-op, I heard my name being called. I looked up and saw Norm waving at me. I waved back at him. It was a nice feeling to be in this strange new world and to know a resident well enough to have him holler "Hello" to me.

At the Co-op, I saw people I didn't normally see on the island. Some were farmers picking up feed; others were just islanders picking out a new shovel. It was never really busy in the urban sense of busy — how busy can a place get when there are only about 100 adults in your community? — but one day there was, dare I say, an actual lineup at the cash desk. I walked in, picked up some vegetables from the produce room, and, as I joined the line, noticed the man behind the counter. He was wearing a Stetson, and I couldn't believe my eyes: he was the actor Nicolas Cage! I tried to stay calm, made it look like I had forgotten something so that I could fall in at the back of the line and really study him. As he bantered with the customers, he even sounded like Cage. But he couldn't be the actor. And the closer I got to the cash register, I realized he wasn't. He was Paul, married to Michelle, Pelee's postmistress.

When I reached the counter, he gave me a huge smile — a big Nicolas Cage smile. "Well, hello there! You must be Jane! We've heard a lot about you!" he said as he stretched his arm across the till to shake my hand.

We had a brief chat, and I kept my nervousness in check. I

still wasn't 100% sold that he wasn't Cage. The resemblance was uncanny.

Over the next few days, as I met people, I casually dropped Paul into the conversation. "Don't you think he looks like Nicolas Cage?" I asked.

"Oh, yeah," they replied. "Everyone says that. Even his wife says that."

Even Sondi concurred when we had lunch that week. She was a good friend of Mrs. Cage and said many tourists had done double takes whenever they walked into the Co-op and saw Paul behind the counter.

Sondi was one of my few neighbours, and I figured it was high time I got to know her. I was one of those city people who could live cheek by jowl with her neighbours and not know them, at least not by name. This was something I wanted to change, so I decided to make a real effort while I was on Pelee.

The first time I saw Sondi was at the airport one day while I was waiting for Ted's plane to arrive. She was with her three little boys in her light blue pickup. A rifle was mounted in the cab, and I deduced it wasn't there for disciplinary reasons — "Johnny, stop that! Don't make me take down that gun!" — but I found the sight rather humorous, especially since Sondi was about the last person you would guess to have a gun. She was a pert, petite blonde — "a babe," as Ted described her once.

Over lunch, Sondi explained emphatically that the gun wasn't there for show, nor was it Craig's, her husband's; it was her gun. She often went hunting after her kids left for school. In fact, she confided, she and Craig had to hunt their dinner one winter when money was rather tight. "We had pheasant almost every night," she said. How exciting, I thought. The pioneer spirit was alive and well at the turn of the millennium.

Sondi, raised in Wapakoneta, Ohio ("the home of Neil Armstrong," she reminded me), had vacationed on the island as a youngster. She had met and married Craig, and the two of them had built a fine home on Pelee. Craig was a Ryersee, a family with a long pedigree on the island. (If you spend any time on Pelee, you quickly realize that people are either Ryersees or McCormicks or descendants of either of those families.)

Now in their early 30s, Sondi and Craig were raising their young family. They were one of the families who had "made a commitment to Pelee," a phrase I heard uttered often on the island in an almost religious tone. I wanted to know how they managed to eke out a living on Pelee given that there were few places to earn money. Sondi replied that she and Craig worked a number of jobs, as did most of the other islanders — on the ferry, as a paramedic-in-training, as guides during the pheasant hunts with their two Labs. Both worked from March to December and had the winters off — an arrangement I found very attractive.

Both Sondi and Craig had postsecondary degrees — she in wildlife management, he in agriculture — and, while she figured they would use those degrees some day, right now they were on Pelee and focusing on their boys. To have the life they wanted meant they had to retool their interests and careers. When both found work on the ferry, Craig earned his captain's papers. Sondi was working toward hers.

The Pelee Project

At that moment, Sondi was my hero. How could I have missed having such a lifestyle myself? I had always wanted to stay home with my children, but I had also felt honour bound, as a modern woman, to go out and earn money so that the pressure wasn't always on my husband to be the provider. I had also thought it was my duty, as a modern woman, to climb the career ladder. I'd had a job from the moment I wrote my final exam at university and, except for maternity leaves, had always been employed. But where had it got me? Unlike Sondi, I could indulge most of my material whims, but at what cost? What also irritated me was how someone so much younger than me had figured this out early in life. How come some people "got it" and others (like me) didn't? I wished I could live my life over and make decisions based on the quality of my life rather than on the elusiveness of some imaginary career quest mapped out by media messages, social expectations, and a myopic women's movement that ignored the richness of a rural life.

But now it was time to turn the tables. Sondi wanted to know what in God's name a city woman with a good job was doing on Pelee Island in the middle of a frigid winter, so I told her my tale.

Pelee Islanders were always curious why I hadn't taken my sabbatical in the summer, when the soft, warm breezes, lush green landscape, and sparkling blue lake made Pelee as close to heaven on Earth as you could get. But the middle of a Canadian winter, when everyone is covered from head to toe in oversized woollen sweaters and socks and burrowed into their homes is really the perfect time for soul-searching work. As the landscape sheds its splendour and is held in suspended animation, there is an instinctive urge to withdraw and study the silence.

I tried to explain this without sounding like I belonged to some half-baked New Age cult. But the islanders were people who, generally speaking, dealt with life in black and white. If I didn't like the city, or felt it was swallowing me up, why didn't I just leave it? Why would I have to come to an island and "think" about it? It wasn't that simple, I explained to them. Once you are seduced by the trappings of urban life, it's difficult to buy back your freedom.

Some of the islanders understood this. George certainly did. He and his wife, Audrey, had been invited to Franny's for dinner this week along with Zoë and me. George and Audrey — so inextricably tied to one another after 55 years of marriage that it was hard to refer to one without naming the other — were the organizers of the Friday lunches at the Legion; they were also heavily involved in keeping Pelee's tiny Anglican congregation from falling into oblivion. The two had met on Pelee when George came over as a supply teacher and Audrey was in grade 12. George, born and raised in Toronto, had later moved to Hamilton (we discovered to our considerable delight that he had attended the same public school — Earl Kitchener — as Zoë). After they married, George and Audrey moved to Leamington, but the promise of a job with Pioneer Seed Company brought them back to the island. They had raised their children on Pelee — all three of whom were now living and working on the island and raising their own families. George knew what I meant when I spoke of the unrelenting stress of urban life. He said he and Audrey needed only to make their once-a-year visit to George's sister in Ottawa, a trip that took them on the hellish Highway 401 along the top of Toronto, to realize they had made the right decision in settling on Pelee. George could relate to my need to get away — so could Franny, who had lived and worked in Philadelphia for almost 30 years and only recently moved to Pelee. In fact, I was discovering that many islanders had done the urban hustle — some of them as far back as the 1940s and 1950s. Even in those relatively benign decades, they had decided the city was too crazy for any sensible human being to handle.

Still, for some islanders the concept of the New Simplicity was foreign, probably because they didn't know there was a New Simplicity; they were still living the Old Simplicity. They knew no other way of life. If what they wanted wasn't on the island, they had to schedule the time and budget the money to travel to the mainland, or they simply had to wait out their desires.

However, the islanders didn't look at their way of life as a means to curb an addiction to shopping; they had chosen Pelee to satisfy a basic human desire: to raise their families in a safe, calm environment and to rely on their own resourcefulness without having their every whim dictated and delivered by a marketing consultant.

My series on nouveau simple living hadn't started running

in the *National Post*, so for all the islanders knew I was just some crazy woman who had landed in their midst and *said* she was writing a series. But it didn't seem to matter to them. We were all getting along very well. Gradually and cautiously, they began to treat me like one of their own.

Chapter 8

A CASE OF CONSUMPTION

*One of the best things about growing old
(or even growing up, for that matter) is the way one gradually
learns to contemplate things without coveting them.*
— *George Faludy*

BANG! My sleepy eyes snapped open at the sound of gunfire.
My God, were we at war? Had the Battle of Pelee Island begun
again?

The Pelee Project

I hopped out of bed and ran downstairs to look out the window. The field across from our house was swarming with men in fluorescent orange vests. A herd of Labs was bounding ahead of them. The winter hunt had begun.

Hunting season is crucial to Pelee. Three two-day hunts in the fall and several hunting days in midwinter inject approximately $1.5 million into the local economy. Full-grown pheasants are released at various points on the island to coincide with the hunting days, and then full-grown hunters are released at various points on the island, and the two sides duke it out. Male executives — mainly from the United States — used the hunts as a kind of company bonding adventure. In the warm months, they packed their golf clubs and went to the links; in the winter, they packed their guns and came to Pelee.

I ran into a number of these hunters at the airport. It was easy to spot the novices getting off the plane; they were the ones wearing neatly pressed khakis and fresh-off-the-rack Eddie Bauer jackets and down vests, looking as if they had stepped off the pages of *GQ.* Some appeared as unaccustomed to holding a gun as they probably were to holding a crepe pan. I never saw a woman among them. I made a mental note to tell Sondi about the untapped niche market in female hunting excursions.

As the hunters blasted their way through our breakfast — Zoë and I found the whole thing pretty comical — I added it to my growing list of Peleeisms. I was falling in love with the quirky sights and sounds of Pelee life, its unmanufactured simplicity, the fact that the entire island fell under the same postal code and the same telephone prefix (you had to memorize only the last four digits in a person's phone number). In major Ontario cities, you have to dial the area code plus a seven-digit number to make a call, even if it is to your next-door neighbour. Pelee's system was the kind of simplicity I liked.

The island had an undeniable calming effect on me, and I felt my real self gaining ground over my unreal self. "Hello!" I wanted to say. "Welcome back!" As a matter of fact, I felt so at home on Pelee, and so at peace with everything and everyone — hey, this retreat thing was really working! — that I decided to check out the local housing market. I wanted to move here — permanently — though how I would pay the mortgage and support myself was a bit of a quandary.

Armed with a laughable bank balance, I called Lou, a local real estate agent. He lived and worked in Leamington, but maintained a home on Pelee that seemed to have its Christmas decorations permanently up. He was only too happy to show me the island. On Saturday morning, Zoë and I piled into his van and headed off to see what was available.

Not too much, as it turned out. Lou mostly drove us past places that had sold recently, giving me the opportunity to kick myself repeatedly for not having stumbled upon Pelee earlier.

Property prices had skyrocketed in the past year due to the recent elimination of a Canadian tax levied on foreign purchasers. With the levy gone, and with the Canadian dollar in free fall, Americans were snapping up properties on Pelee. Capitalizing on this bonanza, a number of Pelee properties were being listed in U.S. dollars.

House hunting with Lou, while informative and very

pleasant, proved to be fruitless, until he offhandedly mentioned a place that was about to be listed. As we drove along a bumpy road, he pointed out the property, so far in the distance and partially hidden by trees that I had to squint to make out its outline. I asked him if we could take a closer look. It meant traversing an even worse road, where the frozen-mud ruts were so deep that we practically had to hold down all our internal organs as we made our way toward the house. Just when it seemed like our kidneys were about to be dislodged, we pulled alongside a two-storey, antique blue clapboard house.

We peered in the windows and walked the property. It was breathtaking. The house faced south and straddled two beaches — two beaches! Lou didn't have the key but said he would locate one and leave it for me at the township office. I could then check out the house at my leisure.

Patience not being my strong suit, I returned to the house the next day with Zoë. As luck would have it, we discovered an unlocked window. I gave her a boost, and she climbed through — not without shrieking "Gross!!!" at least half a dozen times as she made her way to the front door to open the house for my inspection.

The place was a mess — dead flies by the thousands, cigarette butts floating in the toilet, dust and dirt throughout — but the possibilities were endless. So was the view. Huge south-facing windows gave a panoramic view of the lake. To the left was a long sandy beach; to the right, over a few rocks, was another sandy beach, this one bordered by a grove of stately coniferous trees. The main floor had a large living room and an equally spacious dining room, a small kitchen, a bedroom, and a bathroom. Three more large bedrooms were upstairs.

When we returned home, I immediately pulled out some paper and a pencil, then drew the floor plans, reconfiguring the kitchen and the upstairs bedrooms. Within 45 minutes, I had mapped out the renovations, the decorating scheme, and the furniture arrangement for my dream home. I had selected the plants and flower boxes that would adorn the verandah, as well as the colour for the exterior trim. I had everything — except the money to afford it. The house was listed for $300,000; it might as well have been $3,000,000.

Unlikely lessons are found everywhere, and so it was with this cottage. My lusting for it was no different than my lusting for a hundred other things over the years, even when I couldn't afford them — *especially* when I couldn't afford them!

I headed out on my walk to let this sink in. The wind that day had the same bracing effect as a bucket of cold water. Surrendering the object of my newest obsession wasn't easy until I saw it for what it was: a muse for all my past indulgences. I couldn't have the simple life I craved if I continually coveted everything on the planet. After all, simplicity didn't carry a tangible price tag or come packaged in expensive properties. It was at this precise point that I began to let go of material desires and truly changed my buying habits. As I listened to radio reports that the economy was beginning to sag, I felt a tinge of guilt. My about-face wouldn't bode well for North America's financial health.

Not that temptation didn't arrive regularly. Thanks to

The Pelee Project

Canada Post's rerouting system, a number of U.S. mail-order catalogues found their way to my Pelee Island mailbox. Over the years, I had devoured such glossies, mooned over their enticing wares, and, more than once, dialled the oh-so-handy toll-free number to claim my dream. But now, as I leafed through the catalogues, I found myself shaking my head and making absurd statements such as "What kind of person would really want these things?" Gulp! Was that me talking? I flipped through the catalogues again and again, daring myself to find something I wanted. But I couldn't find a thing — not clothing, not furnishings, not even shoes.

While on the mainland a few weeks earlier, I had picked up a couple of decorating magazines. Normally, such magazines were a form of architectural porn for me. They had the ability to whip me into such a lather of decorating fantasies that I required physical restraints. But for the first time, I couldn't find anything that appealed to me. Nothing inspired me. Nothing piqued my creativity. Nothing made me feel like ripping out a room and launching into a redecorating frenzy.

I cast my eyes around Irma's home. Her furnishings — linens, cutlery, dishes — were mismatched, a crime in places where city limits are clearly posted. It was a sharp contrast to my orderly, anal life in which my dish towels matched my wallpaper. Now I revelled in the lack of pretence that character-izes laissez-faire style. Each item in Irma's cutlery drawer was distinct from the others and had an individuality that was intriguing and charming. Why are we so preoccupied with matching everything?

While this change in my values felt comfortable, I worried about how out of step I would be with urban society. I was definitely moving toward the counterculture. I was also on the road to becoming a realist by finally facing the fact that $300,000 homes and cottages weren't for me. Even $600 shoes weren't for me. My money was scarce, and I needed to treat it as such.

This little epiphany didn't deject me at all. It strengthened me. It was OK to admit that something was out of my financial reach. I couldn't have everything, and frankly I didn't want everything. I wanted to make my life easier, not more complicated, and there's nothing more complicated and ultimately more morally worrisome than living beyond your means.

I began to notice other sea-changes in my behaviour. One habit in my urban life that my mother never failed to bring to my attention was my predilection for rushing around creating and fulfilling errands every day. There was always something I needed to pick up at the store. Mom reasoned that half of my self-induced exhaustion could be solved if I just stopped going out. Of course, who listens to mothers? But now I could see she had been absolutely right. I began to plan all my errands around a single weekly car journey — to the Co-op for bottled water, vegetables, and gas; to the post office to mail letters or pick up packages; to the liquor store; to the grocery store; to the dump. If I inadvertently omitted something from my master list or forgot to do something, I did what I rarely allowed myself to do in my urban life: I accepted my forgetfulness and added the missing errand or item to the following week's list.

I started to get a perverse thrill over the fact that my car could stay idle for days and that I could be truly housebound. I began to count the days I didn't use the car, and I became petulant when I was forced to break my streak.

Ted's ban from Pelee Island was lifted this week, and I prepared for his arrival — but not in an obsessive manner. Sure, I cleaned and tidied the house, but I didn't run around with a broom up my rear end like I had done before.

And I conscripted Ted as a helper, something I had always been uncomfortable doing with him or anyone else. Now he was about to become my mainland connection. I cleverly figured out that I could get him to do some minor errands for me so that I didn't have to trek to the mainland myself. I was definitely focused on keeping my expenses in check and spending as little as possible — though you would never have known that from my small accumulation of receipts from Pelee's liquor store.

I called the manager at my bank in Hamilton — I had to explain that there was a place left on this planet that didn't have a bank or a bank machine, a concept she couldn't imagine — and asked her to transfer funds to a branch in Windsor so Ted could retrieve the money and bring it out to me. The wonders of no-branch banking. With cold cash in his hands, Ted was able to pick up a few things for me at his neighbourhood drugstore and grocery store. It was a great saving for me in terms of cost and time. If I kept this up, I could be both house-bound and island-bound.

I was also looking forward to seeing Ted again and to ease some of the tension that had arisen between us. Men don't like being second banana to anything, least of all a spiritual retreat. Plus, Zoë and I were eager to have someone else to talk to at the dinner table each night. When Ted arrived, I made a delicious meal to celebrate the one-month anniversary of our arrival on Pelee soil — roast chicken, roast potatoes, and steamed veggies.

Ted loved Pelee as much as I did, and we began to speak of schemes that would allow us to live on the island full time. After my morning walk — sometimes he joined me — we drove around the island taking in its many splendid sights that the winter landscape had fashioned.

I decided to show Ted the blue house that I couldn't afford. Poor Ted: one minute I was telling him to stay away from me, the next I was dragging him through a $300,000 house.

After a quick tour, he stared at me with a look of incomprehension. "What's to fix up?" he said. "I could live in it just the way it is."

I often wish I didn't hang around people who are so easy to please. They only encourage me.

Deprivation doesn't involve just big-ticket items. When you head down simplicity's path, you find yourself relinquishing not only the big pleasures but also the little, seemingly innocuous ones.

One tenet of the simplicity movement is learning to deal with overconsumption — financial, material, and oral. But it's an almost impossible task when you're seduced every day by posters, billboards, and media advertisements that prey on your insecurities. When you move to a community where none of that exists, you experience a measure of sensory deprivation. It takes getting used to, but you do get used to it. During my first few mornings on Pelee Island, I woke up hyperventilating: There. Is. No. Latte. But like all addictions, it, too, could be tamed.

I began taking pride in the creations from my own kitchen. With a little work and a few ingredients, I could make meals in about the same time it took to go out to the store and buy a frozen entree. It was also healthier and infinitely more satisfying to bring something to the table that I had prepared myself. I savoured the various aromas and took time eating my meals (after decades of racing through meals to meet deadlines or tend to the needs of others).

Even Zoë was impressed by my resourcefulness. This week, for instance, I made cornbread and chicken vegetable soup.

Cornbread: mix 1 cup of flour, 1 ½ teaspoons of baking powder, 1 teaspoon of baking soda, ½ teaspoon of salt, 1 cup of cornmeal, 1 cup of shredded cheddar cheese, 2 eggs, 1 cup of plain yogurt, ¼ cup of vegetable oil, and 1 tablespoon of honey. Mix well and pour into a greased 8-inch square pan. Bake at 425 degrees for 20 minutes or until a knife inserted into the bread comes out clean.

Chicken vegetable soup: put one carcass of a medium-sized

chicken or turkey into a large pot and add enough water to almost cover the carcass. Add in a diced carrot, a diced celery stick, and a chopped onion. Boil well for about 20 minutes and let the mix simmer for about an hour or two. Remove everything except the broth, but save the good bits of meat that have fallen from the bones. At this point, you can either put the covered pot outside in a cool place to let the fat rise to the top or continue making the soup. Usually, it's best to leave it outside overnight. By the morning, the fat will have hardened, and it will be easy to skim off. But for those who are less patient (or less worried about the fat), you can leave the broth on the stove and start making the soup. Chop up two large carrots, two celery stalks, an onion, and four medium-sized potatoes. Add about two cups of chopped-up cooked chicken (including the meat you saved from the broth), two chicken bouillon cubes, a large can of tomatoes, 1 teaspoon of sage, 1 teaspoon of oregano, and 1 $\frac{1}{2}$ teaspoons of basil. Cover and bring to a boil for about 10 minutes, then simmer for an hour or more. Add either a $\frac{1}{2}$ cup of rice or 1 cup of pasta, cover again, and simmer over medium heat for about half an hour. Serve. The soup freezes well.

I rummaged through the box of books I had brought with me. One of them was the *Woman's Home Companion Cook Book*, published in 1942, which I had inherited from my grandmother. In addition to its obvious sentimental value, I love this cookbook because none of its recipes call for culinary exotica such as green peppercorns or Belgium shallots, which are akin to eye of newt in my limited range of expertise. I leafed through it to see what goodies I could concoct.

I hadn't made a meal from scratch in a while; in fact, looking back on it, I realized that, with my long commute and long office hours, it had been a while since I had made an evening meal at all or was home in time to enjoy one with my children.

During our Pelee evenings, as Zoë toiled over her homework or taught me how to play cribbage, I enjoyed a newly acquired luxury: silence. As much as I missed my boys, I was glad they hadn't joined us on this retreat. The petty squabbles, pranks, and bickering between all my children were more than I could handle at times. Their fighting exhausted me. But now the household was quiet, and I imagined my retreat was giving all of us, wherever we were, a well-deserved time-out.

When I brought up the subject of sibling squabbling with Zoë — and she was as much to blame as her brothers for their ongoing battles — she looked rather thoughtful, as if I had jogged her memory about a pleasant occurrence. "But, Mom, brothers and sisters *always* fight."

"You can't honestly enjoy that," I said to her. "Think of all that hitting and punching and the mean words."

A wistful, dreamy smile came over her face as she stared into space: "Oh, but it's so much fun!"

I gave up.

Something else that had been silenced was a few of my more needy friends back home. I was glad I hadn't encouraged them to call me. I had taken on the problems and crises of a few of them, often sacrificing rare opportunities for quiet time so I could attend to their tales of woe. Even going out in the evening with them had become taxing. The conversations had inevitably turned into teary accounts of domestic hell. It had been enough to make me want to cover my ears and run screaming from the restaurant. It's one thing to be compassionate, it's another to spend three or four years listening to the same old rant. Yes, marriage breakdowns are horrible; yes, aging parents are exasperating; yes, it's tough when you don't have a man in your life; blah, blah, blah. Surely there's a statute of limitations on such excessive whining.

My needy friends must have written me off, because I began hearing only from my true friends, who e-mailed me to see how I was doing and to fill me in on what was happening in their busy urban lives and about get-togethers with mutual friends. I wrote back with news about the unlikely pleasures I was discovering, and assured them that I didn't miss shopping, and, no, I wasn't bored yet.

The issue of my boredom was a hot topic among more than a few people, and I began to suspect that some of the islanders thought I would crack under the strain of such a laid-back lifestyle. (I think I had done pretty well since that first day at the Co-op gas pump, and I hoped the bettors were becoming a little less sure of themselves.) Invariably, the first question they asked me after we greeted one another was "Are you bored yet?"

While Jon was slicing some ham for me at McCormick's grocery store this week, he posed that very question to me. I answered him truthfully. Not only was I not bored, but I also found the island kind of busy — what with keeping up with Legion lunches, crafts, movie days for the children, my daily walks, writing, the regular hum of ordinary life. I think he thought I was joking.

But when I visited Paul at the Co-op the same day, he confirmed that Pelee Island didn't always live up to its marketing slogan: Pelee.calm. "Despite what a casual observer might think," he said as he tipped back his Stetson, "this place does have its own rat race."

It was becoming a little impossible to be idle and play the recluse on Pelee. I often think of myself as a bit of a loner, but I am strangely complex in that area because I also experience spurts of gregariousness. It was inevitable, therefore, that my path would intersect this week with that of Mary Lou.

I met Mary Lou while I was out on my seven-kilometre walk, a walk during which I never encountered anyone, except that day. A portion of my route, it turned out, formed part of the route that Mary Lou and her husband, Roger, frequently took. So it was that we trudged toward each other on a long and otherwise deserted road. It was a snowy, bitterly cold morning, and we were all wrapped up in scarves and parkas.

"We wondered whether those footprints belonged to you," Mary Lou smiled, after we shook hands.

I looked down. It had never occurred to me that you could identify someone from footprints. But she was right. There weren't many other footprints around, but when I looked closely I had to agree with her; my boots left distinctive markings. It was while we were immersed in the comparative study of bootprints that I realized she was a witch — not in the "I'll-get-you-my-pretty" sort of way but in a beguiling way. She found insight, and thus inspiration, in the most unusual places and the most unlikely people. I was entranced.

She asked me to come over for tea after I finished my walk. I obeyed and I settled easily into the sofa in her cosy cottage.

It became clear that Mary Lou didn't hide behind her spiritual self — she put that part out front because it was her real self. Most of us do the reverse: we inhabit our various roles, and our spiritual selves languish in the background, even though they may be — for us — our most valuable characteristics. While Mary Lou had many roles — wife, mother, grandmother, friend, drama therapist, hostess, ritualist, mother confessor — none was eclipsed by her sense of spirituality. You always saw her spirit before you saw the role she was playing. That's because she wasn't ashamed of it. In a secular society, it's hard to put forth a spiritual self or even to discuss spiritual issues without being regarded as a bit of a kook. This isn't to say that Mary Lou walked around spouting Bible verses; I don't think I ever heard her utter one, but she always spoke of being "centred," of "self," and she described people who lived off the societal grid as "other."

She also turned out to be as profane as she was pious. I spoke freely with her about the life I had escaped and the one I hoped to find on Pelee. All the changes that I had been experiencing spilled out of my mouth. "Been there, done that," her look seemed to say. She smiled knowingly, matching my observations of our panicky culture with a similar heartfelt experience. She told me that she, too, felt distressed and out of sync with mainstream society. That's why she and Roger had moved to

Pelee Island eight years earlier. She said she had felt a magical pull to be here.

"It's very lonely when you begin to investigate alternative ways to live and when you look beyond your present existence," she assured me.

"I know, but I'm also frightened that what I'm learning is going to further alienate me from the society I live in," I explained. "How far from the mainstream is it safe to go?"

"As far away as you feel comfortable going," she replied serenely.

"But I'm torn between being my own person and being part of a community," I said. "I worry about fitting in when others see me as being so single-minded. In urban life, we're all supposed to walk in lock-step with one another."

"Since when did you give a shit about what other people think of you?" she demanded.

Umm. Since forever?

Our first chat, which I figured would last an hour, went on for three hours — and we still hadn't exhausted our conversation. We had completely lost track of the time.

When I related this to Zoë at dinner that night, she looked perplexed. "How could you not notice the time?" Zoë asked. "You used to always watch the time."

I looked at my wrist and realized I no longer wore my watch. It had been days — or was it weeks? — since I last wore it.

Zoë was my litmus test for change. I was glad when she noticed departures from my normal routines, habits, and perceptions.

I was noticing subtle changes in Zoë too. I had been concerned that she might get homesick, but she didn't. I was impressed at how easily she adapted to island life. My favourite time of the day was 3:45 p.m., when I made a beeline for the living room window so I could watch her return from school. She had an expression of pure joy — a look I had never seen on her face before — as she jumped off the bus and raced to the kitchen door. She looked happy, healthy, and rosy-cheeked here in a rural setting, and she was always bursting with news about her day at school.

I checked in with her teachers to see how she was doing, and it was heartening to hear that she was an excellent student and was getting along with the other children. I got to watch her in action this week when I attended a school event at the Legion on Saturday. The students at PIPS put on a Valentine's Tea, and it seemed as if the entire island was in attendance. The tables were set rather elegantly, and the Legion's bar was groaning under the weight of so many donated goodies. It was fun seeing Zoë interact with everyone effortlessly and without a smidgen of self-consciousness as she poured tea or offered a sweet.

We had found our individual niches and our own group of friends. Both of us were now treated as if we had always lived on the island. As I looked around, I could name almost everyone in the room.

Chapter 9

WALKING THE WALK

Walking is man's best medicine.
— Hippocrates

I was really getting into the swing of things now.

All the petty fears and neuroses that had weighed heavily on me a few weeks earlier had dissipated. It didn't bother me that I wore the same clothes day in and day out or that they were all the same monotonous shade of black or grey. Aside from brushing my hair and brushing my teeth, I forgot about my appearance. I even took my daily walk without lipstick. Au naturel was my maxim. It wasn't a deliberate decision forged from some radical new thinking; it just happened that way. I had better things to do than stand in front of a mirror and draw on my face.

The focal point of my day was my morning walk. I refused to consider any other activity until I had put in a seven-kilometre hike. Of all the changes I was making to my lifestyle, this was one of the biggest. It cleared my mind and helped me to focus on the worry du jour. I could begin the walk mulling over a problem or dilemma and by the end of it, roughly an hour and a quarter later, either solve the issue or declare it to have been not so serious in the first place. I had been walking for the past four weeks — same route, same time, almost every weekday morning. The momentum of the habit had kicked in to the point where it was now second nature.

Patterns and habits are the touchstones of our lives; they give structure to our days and reward us with a small sense of accomplishment. Some people refuse to have a conversation until they've had their morning coffee; others can't begin their day until they've said their prayers, or phoned their mother, or jogged 10 kilometres. The habits of some people are so predictable you can set your watch by them. For Zoë and me, new routines were being established on Pelee.

By week six, I had adapted to the natural rhythm of the day — the physical day, not the manufactured and rushed day. For instance, although we didn't have to wake up until 7:30 on weekdays, I found myself scrambling out of bed a bit earlier to watch the sunrise. If I could get downstairs in front of the dining room window by 7:12, I could enjoy an almost unobstructed view of the sun inching its way up behind a line of trees that framed the field across from our house. I had to be quick; if I was a minute late, the sun would already be on its lazy ascent. But if I was on time, which I usually was, I was treated to a holy moment that always left me in awe. Watching the sun peek over the horizon and spread its rays as if it were having a morning stretch was a sight so glorious I couldn't believe I had spent my life ignoring this remarkable daily occurrence. I could count on one hand the number of sunrises I had seen before coming to Pelee Island, and almost all of them I had observed while on holiday in some tropical climate. Even then I had never fully stopped to marvel at their magic.

But now I was an avid convert — and a bit of an annoying one. On the days I was out and about, I began to tell anyone within earshot about that morning's sunrise; I spoke of it with the kind of authority reserved for discussions on geopolitics. When I encountered people who had the nerve to admit they hadn't noticed that morning's sunrise, I shook my head in a kind but knowing manner that suggested they were in danger of becoming meteorologically illiterate if they didn't pull up their socks.

Zoë and I had slid into a pleasing daily routine. After breakfast, I would give her a quick quiz if she had a test at school that day, and then we would don our winter gear, double-check that her lunch bag was indeed in her knapsack, and, at 8:30, stomp across the crusty, snow-laden yard to the road in front of our house, and wait for the school bus to arrive.

The mornings were cold, crisp, and quiet. As we stood by the side of the road, we would observe the sparse landscape — there were three houses, and acres and acres of flat, frozen fields in our range of vision — and compare it to the urban life we had left behind.

I often thought — and I was sure Zoë did too — about the sights and sounds we would encounter on the street in front of our Hamilton home at that moment. There would be dozens of small troops of chattering, giggling children, knapsacks harnessed firmly to their backs; sometimes Emma, a school chum, would call out to Zoë from across the street, and the two would finish the half-block trek to school together; our street would be clogged with cars and minivans depositing children at the school and then scooting off to far-flung offices; the loud and steady purring of traffic would provide a constant background hum to everyone's well-rehearsed morning choreography; the unmistak-able whistle of Bev, our neighbourhood crossing guard, would pierce the air as she piped the children across Dundurn Street to Earl Kitchener School. Finally, the shrill ring of the school's bell would toll the start of another day.

But on that cold Pelee morning, there was none of that. We saw no one and heard nothing. On most mornings, the sky was a brilliant blue, but it was the stillness and the silence that amazed us. As we waited quietly — afraid to disturb the silence — our icy breaths formed small clouds, like the thought bubbles that accompany characters in cartoon strips. Sometimes we would have a contest to determine who could hear the school bus first, before it came into view about a mile away. The bus would amble to a stop in front of our house, Zoë and I would give each other a nudge that passed as a quick, muted hug ("Don't kiss me in front of the other kids, OK?" she would plead), and she would climb aboard as Grant and I exchanged pleasantries. As the bus moved off, I would wave, and the other school kids would wave back. Then I would turn around and begin my walk.

Our house was located at the southwest corner of East West Road and Curry Dyke Road. I began my walk at that corner, heading south. The first leg of the walk was the most arduous because a fierce wind often blew up from the south; in winter, it was bitterly cold. Zoë had given me a black balaclava for Christmas, and while I wouldn't be caught dead wearing it in the city — I would probably be shot dead for wearing it in the city — I was glad to have it on Pelee. The wind would howl around me and push roughly against me — at times, it was all I could do to move forward — and I would curse this whole walk thing. But I would never turn back: I was afraid the distance I had come was more daunting than the distance I had left to go. Instead, I kept my head down and withdrew into the warmth of my jacket.

As the wind tore by me like cars on an autobahn, I allowed my mind to surf the gamut of emotions: sadness, anxiety, joy, anger, melancholy, rage, loneliness, resentment, elation, worry. I had profound thoughts, hilarious thoughts, and thoughts involving repetitive angst that prompted me to slap myself and say, "For God's sake, get *over* it!" Walking also got the creative juices pumping and enabled me to work through problems, story ideas, dreams for the future, things I should add to my grocery list — you know, the big issues. Unfortunately, the profound thoughts, like my invention of how to get laundry to fold itself, evaporated the moment I reached my door.

When I wasn't thinking great thoughts or indulging in ritual self-evaluation, I surveyed the passing scenery. Curry Dyke Road ends in a T at South Shore Road, and I always turned left. This was my favourite part of the walk for several reasons. First, South Shore Road was, well, the south shore of Pelee, and I revelled in the fact that I was the only person on the planet walking along Canada's most southern shore. Second, the wind would shift dramatically at this point, and I considered this my reward for having survived the brutal trek on Curry Dyke Road. So dramatic was the change in weather that I often took off my balaclava, unravelled my scarf, and unzipped my jacket.

I also loved the south shore because it was, on good days, bustling with wildlife (on bad days, nothing in the wild kingdom — except me — was stupid enough to brave the elements). Squirrels and rabbits bounded through the scrub and slid across the frozen water of the dykes.

Then there were the birds. Birds are no fools, and Pelee Island's winter was too frigid for some of them. But a few hardy species stuck around. They were fun to watch, and sometimes I ascribed urban personalities to them, which wasn't very nice — to the birds, that is.

Zoë is an avid birdwatcher, and she was my teacher in this department. Now, six weeks into my retreat, I could recognize an eastern bluebird (*sialia sialis*), slate-coloured junco (*junco hyemalis*), and brown creeper (*certhia familiaris*). I could even tell the difference between a downy woodpecker (*picoides pubescens*) and a hairy woodpecker (*picoides villosus*). I figured that, by the time I returned to urban life, such sharp-eyed skills would enable me to spot the ubiquitous well-groomed office backstabber (*anus painus*) at 40 paces instead of the usual five.

My route continued past Dick's Marina, where the deserted boat slips stood like abandoned sentinels, past boarded-up cottages, ice-covered rocks, and the vast, frozen lake. On clear days, I could see Middle Island.

I love water, and the south shore was where I indulged my passion for it — even if it was frozen. Lake Erie is the shallowest of the Great Lakes, so it is usually the first to freeze. Huge, jagged ice floes travel all the way from Lake Huron to Lake Erie and freeze in their tracks, turning the lakescape into an ersatz sculpture garden.

The lake never failed to provide something stunning and different every day. On cold, dull days, the sky was a bluish grey that, when juxtaposed with the ice-sculpted waves of Lake Erie, created a tundra-like vista; the next day, the scene and mood could shift dramatically as the rushing of vivid, deep blue water signalled the lake's thaw. Another day, you might encounter a brilliant blue sky and blinding sun reflecting off the snow and ice, forcing you to avert your gaze, as if it was a sight too beautiful to behold. Then there were days when the sunrise, coupled with some well-placed clouds, turned pools of water into the colour of orange sherbet and cast a warm glow

on the blue floes. It was an incredible sight and I felt so peaceful there, I marvelled at how one ordinary scene could have so many variations.

And that was the other reason I so loved being on this stretch of road: it made me feel like me, the real me — loopy, pensive, creative, spontaneous, rigid, devilish, caring, gregarious, withdrawn, gentle, harsh, free-spirited, hard-on-myself, too-critical-of-others, too-compliant, rebellious me. On this stretch of road, I saw myself for what I was: a walking, talking, complex and baffling gene pool, the result of generations of input. People talk about going away to find themselves, and now I had finally found me. It was exciting to finally make my acquaintance — it had only taken 47 years.

The solitude on South Shore Road gave me tons of expressive freedom. I could shout without anyone hearing me, I could cry when a memory stung my sense of pride, I could laugh at one of my hilarious (well, hilarious to me) thoughts, I could talk to myself. I think talking to yourself is very healthy. There's nothing like an intense conversation with yourself to wake you up to the fact that sometimes — sometimes — you *do* have all the answers.

While I relished the solitude, it occasionally worried me. It was such an isolated stretch that I wondered whether I should have brought along a cellphone. I couldn't recall having been anywhere where there was such an absence of people.

I had become naturally protective about my route. One day, I saw Leo's car creeping toward me. Leo was my elderly and exceedingly gentle next-door neighbour, who never failed to respond immediately whenever a mechanical problem occurred in Irma's home. As he rolled down his window, I said, "Hey, what are you doing on my road?"

"Oh, this is *your* road now, is it?" he replied with a chuckle. "I just wanted to make sure you were OK."

I thought that was really nice. People paid attention to the patterns of other people's lives here; I hadn't told Leo that I was walking, but he might have picked it up either from seeing me head off or from a passing comment made by another islander. It was reassuring to know that I wasn't anonymous out here; everyone looked out for one another.

The walk also readjusted my senses. My hearing became more heightened because of the silence. To be outdoors and to hear silence — not nothing, but silence, which are two different things — was wondrous. I could listen to it for hours, and often did.

I heard fissures being formed as the ice gradually splintered on the lake or on the pools of water that formed in the roadside culverts; I heard the water trickle as winter began its thaw. I could hear the tree branches as they moved and knocked against other branches. I could hear the wind blow, and its voice altered with the weather: in cold weather, a soft breeze has a high-pitched tone; on blustery days, it rushes past with a roar; on still days, it is like having someone stand very close to you and breathe gently into your face. The wind was as alive as I was.

During the walk, I could hear the distant buzz of a plane, and in a fairly short time I could distinguish between the plane that brought the mail to the island and the plane that brought the passengers. I became so free-spirited that I often waved to the plane as it prepared for its descent. Once, it flew low enough that I saw the pilot wave back.

My sight was benefiting from the sparse and unobstructed landscape. I could detect subtle movements nearby and on the horizon. On a barren landscape, I was surprised at how much there was to see.

Pelee has an interesting physical history, and I paid attention to it as I continued my walk. At one time, the island was actually three islands separated by large, shallow marshes — Round Marsh, Big Marsh, and Curry Marsh (the area in which I was walking now) — and it remained that way until about 1880, when two Ohio businessmen, Lemuel Brown and John Scudder had the ingenious idea of draining the marshes so that more of the land could be cultivated. With nothing more than shovels and an eager crew — steam-powered dredges proved to be more trouble than they were worth — about 20 kilometres of canals were dug. The water was directed toward three strategically positioned pump houses and then pumped back into the lake. This marvel of engineering doubled the size of Pelee and turned it into an agricultural nirvana. Nutrient-rich soil and a temperate climate like no other in Canada — Pelee Island shares the same latitude with Spain and Italy — ensured a long growing season.

As I continued along South Shore Road, I walked past boarded-up cottages and homes. One such home, recently sold to a Michigan couple, as I learned during my house-hunting expedition the other week with Lou, was Pelee's first customs house, built in 1880. Later, during prohibition, the house was used to export booze overseas.

About the time the customs house was being built, construction was beginning on the Breeze Place Hotel farther down the road. It was a laudable but failed attempt to boost tourism on the island. Set back from the road, it is now a rambling 16-bedroom home. I never saw a person there. Apparently, an Ohio family owns it and uses it for only two weeks in the summer. What a waste: it would make a great spa.

Continuing east, South Shore Road curves north and becomes Stone Road. This was an eerily quiet road, even by Pelee standards. But after South Shore's Street of Dreams, as I called it because I did my best fantasizing there, Stone Road was the Street of Miracles. During my time on Pelee, mysterious and unexplained things happened on this road. Perhaps it was only because my senses were heightened, or maybe it was because I was becoming delusional after hitting the halfway point of my walk, but whatever the reason, this stretch of road was magic. It was also the place where I would find a solution to a problem that I had mulled over during the first part of the walk.

Stone Road is a dirt road and treacherous to walk on because of all the muddy ruts. It's also decidedly less populated than South Shore Road. In fact, there was only one home I passed on Stone Road — the former south-end school, built about 1890 (obviously, there was quite the building boom on Pelee during the late 1800s). At the time, the Ontario government divided the island into four school wards, each with its own school. In later years, this particular schoolhouse served as

Pelee's high school, but dwindling enrolment resulted in its closure. (These days, Pelee's dozen or so high school students are flown to the mainland each week and billeted with families.) The old schoolhouse has since been renovated and converted into a summer home. It's a lovely building, and the separate entrances for boys and girls are still clearly marked. As I walked past it, I imagined what a hive of activity it must have been so many years ago. I could almost hear the ghostly echoes of the children at play.

When I reached the corner of Stone Road and East West Road, I passed a cairn dedicated to the memory of Shaughnessy Cohen, a local Member of Parliament who died suddenly in the House of Commons in 1999. Cohen had a passion for Pelee, her family still maintained a cottage on the island — but the islanders told me the passion hadn't always been mutual. Cohen was not a hunter or a gun enthusiast, and many islanders had blamed her for stalling development that could have improved Pelee's fragile economy. Her cairn marks a 60-acre property — jointly purchased by the rather odd pairing of the Nature Conservancy of Canada and Shell Oil — that aims to preserve globally rare alvar habitat. Alvars are flat limestone plains, remnants of the Ice Age, found only in the Great Lakes and the Baltic Sea.

Turning left at East West Road, I made the final leg back to my home, passing a few more homes, including Gail and Jim's stately Twin Oaks Bed and Breakfast with its gorgeous Victorian wrap-around porch. Along East West Road, I sometimes encountered a car, and my hand would rise reflexively in greeting.

Often the car would pull up beside me, and Dick or Ed or Roger would roll down the window to say "Good morning." If the car came up behind me, I would still wave a greeting before it passed me and before I knew who was driving. This was another Peleeism I learned.

By the time I returned to my home, it was usually about 9:45, and, if I timed it right, I could spy Vicki's little red station wagon. Vicki delivered the mail each day with her mother, Lena.

I happily continued to write my columns for the *National Post*, although the series hadn't yet made its debut. I chronicled my progress on the island, and I filed the stories to my editor by a predetermined weekly deadline.

Aside from having CBC on for much of my day, I wasn't plugged in to much media. CBC was the only Canadian TV station I could get, along with about three American stations. *The Windsor Star* was the only paper the island received. Both of Canada's national newspapers were notably absent. That was about to change.

Since I knew the *National Post* was entering a crucial ratings period, and I knew the paper wanted to increase circulation, and I knew it was holding my series to coincide with the ratings period, and I knew the islanders would want to read about my weekly escapades on their island, and I knew I was missing my daily injection of news (not to mention the horoscopes and the crossword), I called the *Post*'s circulation department in Windsor and convinced the people there to throw a bundle or two of the *Post* in with the daily shipment of the *Star* (the papers were under the same ownership). In their wisdom, they initially sent only three copies of the *Post*, doubting anyone on Pelee Island would read the paper. I found that attitude rather ignorant, and I demanded more papers. Amazingly, my wish was granted. The copies were snapped up by the islanders, and by noon you couldn't sell your soul for one. Initially, the papers were given away free, as is the practice when a newspaper wants to test a new market. Several weeks later, once my series was in full swing, the islanders had to pay for the paper, but at least they now had two from which to choose.

I was certainly getting bullish about Pelee by this time: I thought the islanders deserved better. I began to see examples of the kind of regional disparity that sadly is typical for smaller towns and cities across Canada. Governments put the screws most intensely to these places because the hue and cry is never as loud or carries as much clout as it does in larger cities. Nothing registers in the government or the media unless it happens in Toronto, Ottawa, Vancouver, or Montreal. Everywhere else is deemed trivial.

What really irked me was that Pelee was off the Canadian radar in many ways. And no wonder: it was hard to find a map that had Pelee Island on it, as I had discovered after my first introduction to Pelee. But now I noticed that so-called national news reports, even the one out of Windsor, never even showed Pelee Island on their weather maps. Only a Toledo, Ohio, tv station showed Pelee and most of the 14 islands that populate Lake Erie. Canadians do a disservice to themselves when they neglect little things like this. It's hard to get a country fired up over its national identity and heritage when its people don't know where the country begins and ends. The true boundaries of Canada are Ellesmere Island to the north, Middle Island to the south, the Queen Charlotte Islands to the west, and Newfoundland to the east. Why this is so difficult to illustrate on a weather map is beyond me.

However, my victory in getting newspapers to Pelee Island had worn me out; I decided to leave the broadcasting behemoth for another day. Besides, it was now Friday, and roast beef was being served at the Legion.

Chapter 10

A Visit to Web Hell

For sweetest things turn sourest by their deeds;
Lilies that fester smell far worse than weeds.
— William Shakespeare

My cover was finally blown.

The articles on my lifestyle sabbatical, as it was being called, started running in the *National Post* this week. Suddenly, I was naked. It was one thing to talk about my retreat with family and friends, but now the whole world knew. And my whole world was Pelee Island.

The day the first column appeared, I was preparing for the arrival of the local minister. She was spending the night at our home. If nothing else, I figured my story would be a bit of an icebreaker.

I had briefly met Georgina, the island's Anglican minister, following the two services Zoë and I had attended. Church services on the island were held every other week. The winter's transportation schedule meant that Georgina had to fly from Leamington to Pelee on Saturday afternoon, stay overnight, preach Sunday morning, and take the 4 p.m. plane out that afternoon. Since the church didn't maintain a rectory on the island, Georgina had to depend on the kindness of her flock. All of about five families regularly attended the services, and only two of them regularly took her in: she pretty much bounced between Franny's and George and Audrey's homes.

I wasn't averse to inviting Georgina into our home, I just didn't think she would take me up on the offer so quickly. As Zoë and I were leaving church after our second visit, we exchanged pleasantries with Georgina, and I casually offered our home as a place for her to flop.

"Great!" she enthused. "How 'bout in two weeks?"

"Sure," I stammered, not thinking she would take the invitation seriously. I mean, in urban circles, such invitations are routinely offered but rarely accepted. Georgina didn't trifle with such niceties.

I shot a look at Franny, who hooked her arm through mine

and guided me to my car. "You'll be fiiine," she purred. "She's *very* easy to look after."

I had almost forgotten about the invitation when I bumped into George and Audrey at the Legion the Friday before Georgina was to arrive.

"So Georgina is with you this week," George said to me as I paid for my lunch.

"Umm, yes, she is," I replied, "but I haven't heard from her, so I'm not sure if her plans have changed."

"She doesn't call," said Audrey. "She just arrives, and you pick her up at the airport, and you make sure she gets back to the airport Sunday afternoon."

After the Legion lunch, I returned home and began furiously scrubbing the house, changing the beds, and doing the laundry. Did I have enough food in the house? Would I remember not to swear? What would we talk about? After all, I barely knew her.

Georgina proved to be more than Franny's "easy to look after" summation. She was easier than easy.

I invited Franny and Mary Lou and Roger to join us for dinner, in case we ran out of things to say to each other, but it was readily apparent when I picked up Georgina at the airport on Saturday that there was little chance of that happening. Truth be told, I was a little frantic because I hadn't thrown a dinner party in ages, let alone in someone else's home. I barely knew where the wine glasses were kept, and I debated whether to pull Irma's good china and silver out of hibernation. In the end, I did.

The dinner conversation was lively and bubbled along effortlessly. There wasn't a shy soul among us. Georgina was such an unpretentious and unruffled person that I didn't think twice about throwing her a dish towel when the other guests had left and I had started running the water in the sink. She, in the meantime, had slipped into her PJs and housecoat, and we rounded out the evening with a hot chocolate. I don't think the two of us stopped yakking all weekend.

By the time I came downstairs the next morning, Georgina was already showered and dressed for church . . . in jeans and a sweatshirt. With her supershort hair, she looked ready to lead a hike, not a church service. She did have a bit of lipstick on, though. "Yeah, right, like I'd wear a dress?" she asked rhetorically as she noticed my quizzical expression.

But clothing wasn't the issue that morning. We faced a bigger dilemma. The church service was at 10, but there was also a pancake breakfast at the Legion that began at 9. Could/should we hit the breakfast before the service or after? We decided to go after the church service. "I'll make sure I speak faster during the sermon," Georgina promised.

I had never driven a minister to church, and luckily Georgina wasn't the type who had to be there half an hour before the service started. "As long as I'm there by 10, we're OK," she said. We all piled into my car and headed off on a crisp, icy, but sunny morning. Zoë was quite taken with Georgina, and the two of them chatted easily. I drove, making sure we didn't skid off the road and end up in a ditch.

The church was located at the north end of the island, right beside Pelee Island Public School. It had been built in 1898 as a Methodist church (there were, at one time, four or five denominations represented on Pelee) and was the handsomest of the bunch, fashioned from limestone quarried from the island. It was, Georgina told me, the second Methodist church on the island; the other, smaller one, built in 1882, had been located at the south end. The Methodist population had apparently dwindled quickly, because in 1925 the church was sold to the United Church of Canada. Then, in 1942, the Anglicans took over the church (probably due to a dwindling United congregation), and that, I was told, created a bit of a stink. A few years later, presumably when all the Methodists had left the island, the older and smaller Methodist church was moved to the north end and tacked onto the larger church as its parish hall. The Anglicans had two churches on Pelee: the big Methodist one at the north end, and a much smaller and older (1860s) stone church at the south end. It was used only during the summer months because it wasn't heated. Georgina explained all this carefully to me, but I was baffled by the amount of church-swapping that had gone on on such a tiny island.

We arrived at the church in plenty of time. Georgina headed downstairs to put on her cassock, and Zoë and I slid into a pew beside Franny. The service was spare. There were no thundering organ flourishes or choir or miked minister. There were about a dozen people scattered across the pews. When Georgina spoke, it wasn't like she was speaking to a mass audience — and she wasn't. It was more like a one-on-one chat. And when a dozen scratchy voices (except for Audrey's gorgeous voice) sang the hymns, you could tell we were putting an effort into this moment of fellowship, even though not all of us felt totally comfortable doing so. It was a typical Anglican moment: we're not a herd-type denomination. We prefer solitary spiritualism to group hugs and prayer.

After church, true to her word, Georgina disrobed, and we hightailed it to the Legion for a hearty, cholesterol-laden breakfast. We got home about 1 p.m. and spent the remaining hours gabbing about our respective families, drinking pots of tea, and using Zoë's binoculars to keep track of a bald-headed eagle circling our house.

Georgina and I compared notes on raising teenagers. She told me she and her husband were debating whether to allow their daughter to join the protesters at the upcoming Quebec Summit.

Just before 4 p.m, we drove Georgina to the airport. It had been a wonderful weekend and a great chance to indulge in some gal chat. I asked Georgina to stay with us again, and this time I really meant it.

I spent the next few days writing and dealing with a pile of e-mails. I was amazed at how many people responded to the *Post* articles. The paper ran the series daily for the first week so that, by the end of the week, readers had read six weeks of instalments. There was about a two-week delay between what they were reading and where I was on my journey.

This created a bit of a misunderstanding on the island. My first article chronicled my search for milk and how I knew no one on the island. That evening Audrey and Ruth, another veteran islander, separately showed up at our kitchen door bearing the most incredible goodies: cinnamon buns, a lemon meringue pie, an assortment of homemade jams and cookies. Both women were so apologetic: "We should have done more to help you," they said sadly. "It wasn't proper island hospitality."

"But that was weeks ago," I tried to explain. "The columns aren't appearing in real time. I'm OK now. Really, I am. I know people! I know where to find milk!"

They nodded understandingly, but they left with vexed looks on their faces.

When I wrote about the lack of a hair salon on the island, one islander tore into me via an angry e-mail for not being aware that there was someone on the island who could cut hair.

Each morning, I drove to the West Dock and picked up the paper. It was initially amusing to see a picture of Zoë and me on the front of the newspaper trumpeting the latest Pelee instalment, but by day three amusement turned to indifference. What I didn't know was that the series had struck a chord with readers across the country — and beyond. My mother phoned to tell me that Zoë and I had become minor celebrities: no less an august group than her bridge club was avidly following our adventures, she reported, adding as an aside that our retreat was being discussed on radio talk shows. Friends e-mailed and phoned to say the series was being debated at dinner parties, at office water coolers, and in coffee shops.

The *Post* urged me to log on to the website it had set up for the series and to respond to readers' comments. The paper had put a tag at the end of my columns saying that I would be "hosting" an on-line discussion. Hosting made it sound so civilized, but in fact it was like a barroom brawl in that chat room. After making this technological leap, I almost immediately regretted getting involved.

There were loads of wonderful, heartfelt comments as well as measured comments from naysayers who found my series intriguing but doubted I would stick it out. I was puzzled that people considered my retreat an endurance test. Then there were the sluggers. I was roused from my New Simplicity inertia and came out swinging.

I was lambasted for having bought expensive shoes, and my Manolos became a lightning rod among the bitter class. The *Post* always boasted about its upscale demographic, but obviously those upscale readers weren't logging on to the website. Those who were objected mightily to someone spending $600 on shoes.

At first, my bad urban reflexes resurfaced. I wrote angry responses to those who criticized me and told them I didn't give a rat's ass what they thought about my journey or my shoes. Naturally, I blew it. Here I was, Ms. Benign Simplicity, and I was behaving in an entirely unbenign way. Why was I being so defensive? Why was it so hard to accept that not everyone would agree with me?

By the time I logged off, I was beaten, bruised, and embattled. What's more, some of those comments had come from islanders, and I felt hurt and misunderstood. I tried to engage them in a cyber discussion, but I came off sounding shrill. One islander, whom I had never met, posted a message on the website alerting readers that, based on the tone of one of my e-mails to her, I really was "a Toronto bitch." I hadn't thought there was anything wrong with my "tone," but the episode taught me an important lesson on how mail — cyber or otherwise — can be misinterpreted when you are writing to someone who doesn't know your real voice. (I resisted the urge to tell the author of that missive that, for her information, "bitch" was an acronym for Babe in Total Control of Herself.)

A Vancouver contributor to the website told me he had received an angry e-mail from one of my relatives telling him what a wicked person I was. The e-mail was so vicious, this reader confided, that he was going to stop writing to me.

On top of all this, I got a call a few days later from one of my ex-husbands, who, at the end of a long barrage of criticism, said, "And by the way, everyone hates you, you know. Just read your website." I could have died. I was so upset that I didn't know what to do. Actually, I did know what to do, but it was illegal.

Instead, I threw on my jacket and went for a walk around the block to blow off some steam. I thought of all the yet-to-be published columns and prepared for the ensuing torrent of bitter mail: my need for a pedicure, the lack of a spa, my complaints about the clothing I had brought, my lament over no chi-chi coffee now sounded trivial, snobbish, and whiny. And they were. But I was weeks ahead of what people were reading, and I implored them to stick with the adventure, because transformation of any real kind doesn't occur overnight.

This is an exasperating aspect of our society — everyone wants a quick fix. We have become so accustomed to having our problems solved, our lives realigned, our perceptions altered in one neat magazine article, TV sitcom, or talk show that no one has the attention span to stick with longer journeys. People want their problems fixed instantly. We are urged to walk faster, talk faster, work faster, do everything faster. If you pause to consider what you're doing, you are deemed slow and indecisive. But try telling that to someone fixated on a pair of $600 pumps.

I was able to expend some more of my angst a few days later. I was just about to put out a load of laundry when Sondi called me and asked if I wanted to go hunting with her that morning.

Would I?

An hour later, Sondi arrived toting her gun — a gleaming 20-gauge shotgun. I had never experienced gun envy before. I told her about a .22-calibre rifle I once owned, but she scoffed at the mention of it. She was way beyond such sissy guns.

Sondi said she didn't shoot for sport, and for that reason we wouldn't shoot rabbits or foxes. With her Labs in tow, we stomped across the fields of wheat stubble toward a distant treeline.

"You're quite the celebrity here," she said. "Everyone's talking about you."

"Nice things?" I asked.

"Well, they're curious," she replied cautiously.

I wondered whether "curious" was code for "bad things."

It was great to be outdoors. It was wickedly cold, but it was nice to escape from web hell and spend time with someone pleasant, even if she was holding a gun.

Sondi and I talked about our respective histories, our children, our lives — so different, and yet our dreams so similar. That's the irony of the human condition: we all try to attain the same goal, but we chart different paths to get there.

Our conversation then turned to hunting. Sondi said she only shoots what she can eat, primarily pheasant. She even had a culinary tip: "Pheasant only needs about half an hour in the oven. Most people really overcook them."

I nodded in agreement, remembering a pheasant I had cooked several months earlier. When I pulled it from the oven, the species had to be confirmed through dental records.

An hour and a half later, we were back at my house, chilled to the bone and empty-handed. Sondi handed me her gun and asked me to shoot off the cartridge she had loaded into it.

"Where?" I asked.

"Wherever," she shrugged, looking around at the deserted, open terrain.

I thought of my website but took aim at the empty field, and immediately her dogs moved into range. Great. I raised the gun higher, above the treeline, and fired. The gun jerked in my arms, and the force of the blast almost knocked me off my feet. "It's got quite a kick," I smiled, embarrassed, regaining my balance and handing the gun back to her.

"Shoot some more," she ordered.

I gamely blasted another shell into oblivion, no steadier on my feet than I had been with the first shot. I was out of my depth but only temporarily. I decided I wanted to learn how to handle a gun, and I asked Sondi if she could take me to the island's

Sportsman's Club so I could try my hand at trap shooting.

That's what I liked about Pelee women: they can do their nails, chop wood, hunt a pheasant, and cook it up all on the same day. They weren't girly girls clutching water bottles or low-fat triple frappuccinos and fretting over their next gym session. They were hardy, healthy gals who weren't afraid to throw their heads back in laughter or stomp through the woods toting a gun.

Back at the homestead, I mellowed a bit on the nastier web mail (I don't know what I would have done without a liquor store on the island). I focused on the positive mail and phone calls I received, which far outweighed the bad ones. I shared them with Zoë so she didn't think I was a complete loser.

A by-product of our newfound celebrity status was receiving phone calls from total strangers. One such call came from a couple who had a weekend home on Pelee. They called me up in a fit of laughter, having apparently just read one of my columns, and spoke to me as if I was a long-lost friend. They said they were coming to the island that weekend and insisted Zoë and I join them for dinner.

I eagerly accepted the invitation because, well, you never know how serendipity works. However, it was clear when we arrived at their house that our hosts had already been heavily into the serendipity. They were riotous and kept trying to get Zoë and me to dance. At the end of an excruciatingly late dinner, the hostess dropped her head into her dinner plate and fell asleep.

"Were they drunk?" Zoë asked as we sped away in our car.

"Just a little high-spirited," I replied tactfully.

Chapter 11

THE ARRIVAL OF "MRS. GOT-ROCKS"

A mother, who is really a mother, is never free.
— Honoré de Balzac

"The next time you decide to run away, choose Paris or New York."

Those were the first words my mother spoke as she set foot on Pelee Island's tarmac, having just disembarked from a seven-minute plane trip that, sadly for me, lacked an in-flight bar service.

The Pelee Project

Even though she had travelled all over the world, Mom had never been to Pelee Island, and the trip had stumped her about what to pack. She couldn't fathom a place where people didn't dress up, and, perhaps more to the point, she couldn't imagine that I could live in such a place. I had told Mom to dress casually, but there's no telling a mother anything. Claiming she didn't own anything casual, she stepped off the plane bedecked in pearls, gold necklaces, a skirt and blouse, mohair coat, and full makeup, which made those of us who approached the plane look like squeegee kids, minus the squeegee and the swagger. In fact, it was impossible to swagger with a bitter winter wind buffeting our heads. The wind had been so bad that it had forced the cancellation of the flight the day before, and Mom had spent the night in Leamington — another first for her. She had taken the inconvenience in stride, and I think it had heightened the island's mystique for her. But now that she was here, and had hurriedly sized up Pelee's flat, bleak terrain, she needed a Scotch.

As Zoë and Mom hugged each other, I got the car and drove it out to the plane to pick up Mother's luggage. Since she wasn't dressed lightly, I expected she wasn't travelling lightly either. And I was right. Since her daughter and granddaughter were out in the middle of a lake in the dead of winter, she had figured it was only a matter of time before Zoë and I succumbed to cannibalism, so she had brought along a crate of groceries.

It was exciting for Zoë and me to get a chance to play island host for a change. As we drove Mom back to our home, we pointed out the sights along the way: a small vineyard that produced exclusively for a French winery; a model replica of Vin Villa, one of the architectural beauties of the island, which had mysteriously been torched in the 1960s; the white clapboard Roman Catholic church; and then our home.

We got Mom settled, poured her a Scotch, and sat down to chat. We hadn't seen one another since Christmas, so we had a lot to catch up on. She filled me in on what was happening in her world — our family, her friends, her various outings — and I told her about Zoë's progress in school and how we were adapting to Pelee life.

Then I asked the question I was dying to ask her. That week marked the halfway point — Zoë and I had been on the island 50 days — and I wanted to know if Mom noticed a change in me. Mom looked at me and then at the clock. "Oh! It's almost time for *Oprah!*" she said with excited relief. Clearly, she wasn't ready to present her verdict. We switched on the TV.

Despite the long weeks of solitude, I had watched little television. Besides, I was enjoying the silent moments of my day and sought out quiet pursuits. I loved silence. I craved silence. I began to wonder whether there was a silent religious order on the planet that accepted burnt-out mothers as nuns. Maybe I could start one. Talk about your niche market.

But when Mom picked up the channel changer, I knew silence would be an elusive goal that week. As a senior in denial, she required the TV on at the highest decibel level known to humans, a level that nearly shattered my now delicate eardrums after weeks without fighting children, honking horns, screeching tires, and grocery buggies being slammed into their parking pen. The TV was so abrasive it made Dr. Phil sound like Dr. Dre.

The next morning, after Zoë went off to school, I told Mom I was heading out for my seven-kilometre walk and that I would be home in an hour.

"You'd better take this," she said, handing me her cane. "Just in case."

"Just in case what?" I asked, truly perplexed. Would a rabbit jump at my jugular? A cormorant crap on my head? I told her that it was totally unnecessary. I told her that we never even locked our doors.

She freaked out and told me that such behaviour was just tempting fate.

I stood my ground: I was *not* taking a cane on my walk.

That afternoon my cousin Ann joined our little house party. She had taken a week off from her retail job in London, Ontario, and wanted to see, firsthand, what the Pelee buzz was all about. Ann, too, brought groceries and goodies as well as her little mutt, Butch. Zoë was in heaven with so many of her favourite women around.

I stuck to what was left of my routine. Ann joined me for my morning walk, and it was fun to have her company. But the big bonus in having house guests was pulling out the stops and seeing the sights of Pelee — in the middle of winter.

One of our tourist stops was the Pelee Club. Dave, the club's handsome, young custodian, was wonderful about letting us see inside a building that was normally off limits to the public. He had been repainting the interior, and, frankly, I think the paint fumes were getting to him. The chance to play tour guide was a bit of a relief for him.

With three women — all of us history buffs — hanging on his every word, Dave was in his element. The Pelee Club, he told us, had an auspicious birth. About 1880, a group of rich American buddies decided to make their annual Pelee fishing trip more permanent. They purchased 10 acres of woodland at the northwest corner of the island and built a cavernous 40-room lodge. Membership in the club was limited to a select group of 25 people. We noticed some impressive names in the club's guest book; its founders were listed — Marshall Field, General Philip Sheridan, Judge Walter Gresham, Robert Lincoln (a descendant of Abraham Lincoln) — as were some guests, such as Grover Cleveland and Howard Taft. The building was prefabricated by one of the members, George Pullman, of the Pullman train fame, whom I imagined would be pretty handy to have as a member of any club.

As we walked through the clubhouse, Dave pointed out some of the furniture — beds and dressers — that Pullman had built. For a lodge that was supposed to be a place to kick back in, the furniture was none too shabby. Within minutes, Mom, Ann, and I started picking out our rooms.

The bar area was large but cosy, and an adjoining screened porch overlooked Lake Erie. Upstairs was a billiard room and some rather deluxe bedroom suites. There was even a bowling alley on the grounds, though the lanes had become warped over time. The club hadn't planned for the bowling alley to be a permanent fixture, and a foundation was never built for it.

All in all, the Pelee Club had the makings of a first-class hotel, but the place was rarely used. It was a beautiful, sunny day — not a speck of snow anywhere — so we walked the grounds and gazed at this cream and green-trimmed marvel, shaking our heads at the wasted potential of such a place (I stubbornly refused to give up the spa idea).

We waved good-bye to Dave and set off to check out another historic building he had recommended. We soon arrived at the imposing limestone structure that was once the home of Sarah Ann McCormick, daughter of Pelee's first owner, William McCormick. It was constructed on land belonging to the McCormick homestead farm.

The house had a cornerstone that read "1895: Except the Lord build the house their labour is but lost that built it." Its meaning made little sense to us until we consulted a modern-language Bible that night for a translation: "Unless the Lord builds a house, the work of the builders is useless." Oh, OK, we got it. Still, it was a curious sentiment to affix to a house.

Sarah's motives for building the house in the first place were equally curious. One of 12 McCormick children, Sarah never married (half of that brood didn't) and built the house when she was well into her 60s. She died three years later.

Back on the main road, Mom, Ann, and I stopped the car at Vin Villa and surveyed the haunting ruins of this once stunning estate. Vin Villa was built by two men from Kentucky who purchased a 25-acre parcel from William McCormick (there's that name again) to start a vineyard in 1866. It flourished, and a stone mansion-cum-winery was erected. A wine cellar was excavated out of the rocky ground, and when it was finished it measured an astounding 60 feet by 40 feet and 12 feet high. Above it was a basement, amazingly the same size as the cellar, and it served as the winery. Its entrances were large enough that a horse-drawn cart groaning with grapes could easily clear the doorway. Above the basement was built a storey-and-a-half home in the style of a southern mansion.

Over the years, the home was lovingly maintained and furnished with terrific antiques. But eventually no one returned to Vin Villa, and the house, though boarded up, was frequently invaded by teenagers. (Someone I met on the island admitted that, in her youth, she had wandered through Vin Villa, and she verified that the joint had indeed been stunning, both in its architecture and in its furnishings. So immaculate and family-ready had Vin Villa been that she had expected someone to walk through the door at any minute. Mountains of antiques had been left unclaimed, a fact that made Mom salivate.) In time, vandals got the better of Vin Villa, and according to several islanders more than a few Pelee homes eventually contained Vin Villa furnishings. In the late 1960s, someone torched the place. The flames were reportedly so extensive they could be seen all the way from Ohio.

(I must confess that while strolling the grounds one day during my winter retreat a sudden terror seized me, and I got the sense that something evil and gruesome had taken place on the Vin Villa site. I don't often get sensations like that, but it was strong enough that I called out to Ted, who was busy shooting off a roll of film, and told him we had to leave the place — *immediately*.)

Our travelling trio resumed the tour, and we drove past Pelee's cemetery, agreeing to check it out the following day, which, of course, we never did. I showed Mom and Ann our church, the school Zoë attended, Franny's home, the lovely stone Regency cottage built in 1847 by Alexander McCormick (son of William), the former island grocery store (circa 1890, now the Scudder Bar & Grill), a fabulous log home thought to have been built about 1830. . . . Then it was time for a Scotch and *Oprah*.

The next day, when I thought that Mom would spontaneously combust without a shop in which to prowl, I called Dick, who owns the Trading Post, and Aurella, who owns Down the Lane clothing boutique, and begged them to open their stores for an hour. They said to come by on Friday.

It was during lunch that Mom slowly waded in with her assessment of me. But I had to interrupt her. I had spotted Paul, the fellow from the Co-op, outside filling up my oil tank.

"Excuse me," I said, getting up from the table. "I just want to say hello." Then, turning to Ann, I said, "Take a look at this guy. He's the spitting image of Nicolas Cage."

"Who the hell is Nicolas Cage?" Mom asked.

I walked outside to see Paul. It was cold, and I offered him a tea, but he said no thanks. We chatted for a minute, and I asked him to say hello to his wife, Michelle, for me. Then I went back inside.

When I returned to the dining room table, Ann's eyes were wide. "Oh. My. God. That *is* Nicolas Cage!" she said.

"It's uncanny, isn't it?" I said, recounting my first meeting with him at the Co-op.

Mom still didn't know who Nicolas Cage was. Then she spoke.

"You have changed, Jane," she said. "You seem so happy. And you never used to be so friendly to people. You don't even do that little thing you always did after you talked to people."

"What thing?" I asked.

"You know, the way you used to talk to people, then turn around, roll your eyes, and give that little snort."

Did I?

"Now you really take time with people, even strangers," she continued.

"But they aren't strangers," I said. "They're friends."

"But two months ago you didn't know these people existed," she insisted. "Now you're so easy with them."

I told her I felt like I had found my tribe, a sentiment articulated to me by Mary Lou the week before. It so perfectly described the comfortable bond I felt with the islanders. They did seem like my people. We all came from different walks of life and had different life experiences; some people were funny, some were serious; some were educated, some were not; some were boisterous, some were not; some were spiritual, some were not. Yet we connected effortlessly with one another. What was our common denominator? Was it because the island had beckoned us individually? Was it because we had been cut from the same cloth in the sense that we were willing to trade many of our comforts to live life off the urban grid? Were we searching for a life that offered something more than the usual grind? Life can be hard and dreary, no matter where you live, but there was a quality of life on the island that was hard to pass up.

The "tribe" comment didn't sit well with Mom. She took it to mean that I was distancing myself from my biological family. That certainly wasn't the case, but it did make me wonder why we feel so attached to certain strangers and so alienated from certain blood relatives. I've attended family gatherings and, looking around, asked myself, "Was I adopted?" Although my relatives are fine people, we have little in common other than our lineage. To avoid the possibility of either Mom or me saying something that might unintentionally hurt the other, we hastily flicked on *Oprah*. Maybe we could divine some insight from Ms. Winfrey.

After that, it was time to get ready for dinner at Dan's. Dan was a new addition to my Pelee coterie. A few weeks earlier, he had phoned me and introduced himself, saying he had heard about me from Dick. He said he was "starved for intelligent conversation" and asked me when I could come over. I stammered, as people with totally empty social calendars do, and suggested we get together the following week, which is how it's done in the urban world.

"Next week?" he asked incredulously. "Well, what are you doing *now*?"

"Waiting for my daughter to come home from school," I replied.

"When's that?" he asked.

"About 4 p.m.," I answered.

"Good, then I'll see you about 4." He hung up.

Our first visit at Dan's was delightful. Zoë fell in love with his black Lab, Apollo. Dan had hundreds of stories befitting a man whose work had included owning homes all over the world and whose engineering firm had worked with the royal families of Saudi Arabia. His wife was at their other home — in Málaga — but Dan had decided that this winter he needed the solitude of Pelee more than the social whirl of Spain. He was a gracious host, and when I mentioned that my mother was going to be visiting Pelee, he insisted I bring her for dinner.

Ann wasn't feeling well that night, so she stayed home, but Mom, Zoë, and I spent the evening with Dan, his niece Judy, Mo, the island's irascible nurse, and Trading Post Dick. Dan's sprawling home on the water's edge was the cosiest and most convivial place to be on that cold, dark, blustery night. Dan had Scotch and the same politics as my mother, so the two of them hit it off. She didn't even notice that we were out on a school night.

The next day, my guests capped off their visit with lunch at the Legion, a gander through the Trading Post and Down the Lane, and then afternoon drinks at Franny's. When we arrived at Franny's, we ran into Zane, who was checking his sap buckets. He had tapped the maple trees on Franny's property and had already made a few bottles of maple syrup, which he was selling for $15 a bottle at McCormick's grocery store. Each of us had bought a bottle. Sure it was pricey, but who could resist Pelee Island-made maple syrup in a bottle shaped like a maple leaf? I introduced Mom to Zane, who winked hello to her, a gesture my mother found rather flirtatious.

"Relax," I told her. "People here are just as likely to wink at you as tell you to screw off."

Being Scotch gals, Franny and Mom got along well. Mom had heard a lot about Franny during her time on the island, including the rumour that she was the richest woman on Pelee, which Franny vehemently denied. Maybe she was just one of those women who *look* rich. Anyway, she deftly managed to deflect the rumour by zeroing in on Mom's flashy jewellery and mohair coat, and she christened her "Mrs. Got-Rocks." Mom refused to dress down on an island that refuses to dress up.

Bright and early the next morning, I put Mom and Ann on the plane back to the mainland. Mom reiterated her comments about seeing a change in me, but she added that she was reserving judgment until I was back in the bosom of the Golden Horseshoe's big money and bright lights. She figured I would be waving my credit card the moment I saw streetlights again. It was a fair comment, but I told her I would prove her wrong. After 50 days of self-imposed penury, I had lost my lust for luxury. We hugged and kissed good-bye.

As enjoyable as the visit had been, it had also been exhausting. I had been jerked away from my meditative routine, but I was proud of the fact that familiar faces hadn't made me regress into my old habits. And Mom had noticed a difference in me, so I was indeed making progress.

Still, I couldn't quite yet return to my reclusive-wannabe lifestyle. I was expected at Blueberry Hill at 4:30 that afternoon for drinks — Georgina was staying with Franny for the weekend — and then we were going to the Legion for a special Chinese dinner. After that, I had to finish preparing a lesson for next day's Sunday school. Sondi, who regularly performed this duty, had gone to Florida with her family for a holiday. I had offered to fill in for her. She gave me the week's lesson and told me to check out a website for a craft to go along with it. Who knew you could find an entire site devoted to Sunday school lessons and crafts?

I was worried that I wouldn't be able to explain the lesson clearly, that the King James version would be too difficult for my young charges. So when Zoë and I got to Franny's, I asked if Franny or Georgina had a modern translation of the Bible that I could borrow.

And that's when serendipity popped in. Neither Franny nor Georgina could help me, but a voice from above offered me a Bible. I looked up, and peering over the loft railing were Melissa and Shawn, a young couple from Windsor who were weekend guests at Blueberry Hill. Without hesitating, Shawn offered me his Bible: it was so new that it still had that new-Bible smell. I couldn't believe someone I had never met would lend me something so precious, so freely. I thanked him and promised to return it the next day after church.

Interestingly, the passage I was to teach was from Psalm 91:11: "For God will order his angels to protect you wherever you go." It was becoming clear that all sorts of angels had been sent to guide and teach Zoë and me wherever we went on this rather mystical little island.

The Pelee Project

I needn't have fretted about Sunday school. Two of my little charges erupted in tears within minutes — the darling tykes missed their mom — so, as a diversionary tactic, I quickly launched into the craft du jour.

Chapter 12

The Ladies of Lent

For my part, I know nothing with any certainty,
but the sight of stars makes me dream.
— Vincent van Gogh

Now, where was I?

The previous week with Mom and Ann had been such a whirl of activity that I was left a little discombobulated about my routine and my new purpose in life. Oh, yeah, I'm supposed to be seeking spiritual enlightenment, adopting a simpler, less chaotic life, and writing a weekly column about them.

I sat down at my computer and started banging off another instalment (mothers manage to provide a rich vein of material). I also checked my e-mail and felt sufficiently brave and confident to venture into the website to see what fresh furor my columns had elicited.

I felt more adept at handling the letters now. People were entitled to their opinions, after all. Some readers didn't have the patience for the journey; they wanted to know *now* what my decision would be. Some actually wanted me to tell them how my retreat would end. They wanted the reassurance that life could be neatly tied up into a manageable package with a bright red bow on it. It was further proof that patience in our society is a rare commodity.

I replied to all my readers, whether they were for or against me. It threw me off at first that total strangers found it necessary to weigh in on my private life. But I had asked for it: I had put myself on public display, and I had to take the lumps with the love. I figured such an intrusion was a small price to pay to get my soul back.

The more caustic e-mails were hard for Zoë to understand. She was getting teased at school, and she took the comments levelled against me — especially those from anonymous islanders — personally. I told her she couldn't expect to win over everyone in the world, not even family members — sometimes *especially* family members. I also told her there must be a good reason for a person's anger. We shouldn't always blame people for their actions against us; sometimes we bring anger on ourselves because of what we said or did, whether it was intentional or not. It was a lesson, I told Zoë, in being mindful of never leaving a wrong impression.

Of course, it was totally unlike me to dispense such measured advice. I possess many traits, but a cool head isn't one of them. But there on that dark night, on a silent island, in the middle of a frozen lake, the answer seemed simple and clear: when we fight back, we further the aggression, first, by engaging in the fight and, second, by giving the other person additional ammunition. When we raise our voices, we incite anger. When we dig in our heels about something — even if they are only princess heels — we set the stage for intractable combat, both real and perceived.

I felt a rush of understanding wash over me: this was an epiphany. It was like figuring out Rubik's cube. Now I got it: if I stopped arguing with people, maybe they would stop arguing too. If I didn't always take the defensive, perhaps the outcome would be less offensive. If I stopped pouring my energy into excuses or trying to prove I was right all the time, maybe others would let up. I decided to test the theory.

The following morning, after Zoë left for school, I phoned one of my ex-husbands. Poor guy. I knew the mere sound of my voice would immediately raise his blood pressure. I was right. Within seconds, he launched into his familiar, venomous diatribe about my lousy parenting skills, my lousy life skills, and my lousy personality.

I let him finish. And then I said, "You're right. I have been wrong. I have not been as good a parent as I thought I was. I've really made some bad mistakes, and I'm so sorry. Can you tell me how I can do better?"

There was a pause as he scrambled to collect himself from the shock of this admission. But he continued. "And another thing. . . ."

Again I let him finish. And again I said, "You're right. Please, how can I make this better?"

That's about all it took to take the wind out of his sails. There really *is* power in letting go. By the end of our conversation, the atmosphere had settled down, and we said good-bye on a pleasant note. My willingness to accept the blame — and humbly, to boot — diffused his need to lash out at me. As I zipped up my jacket and headed out on my morning walk, I sensed a surge of pride at having not only decoded an area of human relations but also having put it into practice.

Although I am not a bad parent — I think in some ways I've been an admirable parent — my ex-husband had a different take on things, and no amount of arguing was going to convince him otherwise. Possibly, I had done something long ago — maybe even unintentionally — to provoke his opinion of me. Perhaps he had magnified one or two episodes that coloured his perception of me. That was OK. Often the only way we can change others' perceptions of us is through our deeds, not our words. It may take decades, not days, to prove our sincerity. Even then, our adversaries may choose to ignore us as we try to improve. But we should continue to improve ourselves for our *own* sake, not for the benefit of others.

Spitting matches aren't worth the energy needed to maintain a defensive dance with someone. If the other person shows no sign of budging on a point, then it falls to you to diffuse the situation, even if it means conceding defeat. When you think about it, it takes more bravery to concede defeat graciously than it does to slam another medal on your breast and walk around with a goofy, self-congratulatory grin on your face. Plus, there's humility in defeat, and we could all use a bigger dose of that from time to time.

However, such a tack is contingent on one party sacrificing ego and comfort level. Admitting you are wrong stings, but the aftereffects can be euphoric. Even academic evidence bears this out. A study at Hope College in Holland, Michigan, found that those who are able to forgive the people who have wronged them are healthier than those who harbour grudges. I imagined the lengths to which I could take this: perhaps I could become a mediator extraordinaire and solve the world's problems.

As I looked out at the steel blue water of Lake Erie from South Shore Road, I shook that fantasy out of my brain and decided instead to make a quick list of everyone who had a grudge against me. I would try my grand experiment on them. But as the list grew, I realized I didn't have enough money to pay for all those long-distance calls. Besides, saying you're wrong once to someone is enough humility for one day. Like victory — or is it revenge? — humility is something to be savoured.

Zoë and I were solidly in the Pelee groove. We felt completely at home. But every so often my eyes drifted toward the calendar, and I began calculating the end of our retreat. I knew we had to go back to urban life, where there was the promise of a full-time paycheque. Living on a freelance wage had its limits, even when one was pursuing a simple life.

The thought of leaving Pelee Island was hard to accept. I dissolved into tears whenever I drove along the quiet roads. In some ways, I felt as if I was just beginning my journey; in other ways, I felt as if I had lived here all my life. What was so compelling about this place that it reduced me to tears? It was such a polar opposite of the life I had led up to that point. And I was learning real life lessons here, not mindless lessons like how to inject more RAM (whatever that is) into your computer or how to faux finish a piece of furniture.

I was meeting plenty of people who seemed to have mastered those life lessons. Mysteriously, I hadn't been given the manual at the beginning of my life. I was a late bloomer, and now I was playing catch-up.

People continued to ask me if I was counting the days until my next shopping expedition. But I wasn't. I didn't miss any of the trappings of city life. Those very trappings had kept me tethered to a material life and disconnected from an authentic one. I was free, and having tasted real freedom I wasn't about to trade it or give it up. Finally, after decades of searching, I was able to lead a life I felt comfortable with. Why had it taken me so long to find it? Was I so different from other people that I couldn't see what everyone else seemed to grasp so easily? Was the desire to find true life more important to me than it was to other people?

I was chided by those from my urban life about returning to "the real world," but I had a ready retort. "This *is* the real world," I told them. "You're the one living in the unreal world. Actually, your world is surreal." Of course, they didn't get it. How could they? They were constantly subjected to a pounding of hype and histrionics and weren't strong enough to pull away from it. Some admitted as much: "I could never do what you're doing. It would be too weird."

But others didn't find it weird. They understood the urge to break free of society's shackles. They even wanted to do it themselves. But they knew it would come at a price they weren't prepared to pay.

One woman following my series in the newspaper emailed that she had shown my articles to her husband, who had immediately scoffed at them. Thanks, buddy. His wife was yearning to talk to him about her desires and dreams, but he wouldn't even consider a discussion on the subject. He laughed off the idea of a lifestyle sabbatical as being "flaky." The woman thanked me for letting her at least know that such retreats were possible and that she wasn't alone in wanting one.

Not all the mail I received was electronic. In my rural mailbox, letters arrived whimsically addressed to Jane Christmas, Serenity Lane, Pelee Island, Ontario. Some were notes of encouragement, while some were letters from islanders who were living on the mainland during the winter and who found the sudden interest in Pelee Island amusing. Mary Ann, a business associate of mine, sent Zoë and me a box of pistachios, which we devoured, I'm ashamed to admit, like crazed animals. Other people sent Bible passages or book excerpts they thought I would find inspiring. I cherished this soulful connection with strangers, and I felt my heart thaw. It takes real courage to write to a stranger and confide your private thoughts.

Although Zoë didn't talk much about such things, I could see a change in her. She adapted to the island faster than I did, I think, and seeing her move within our new world with such ease boosted me. She was less competitive than she had been in our urban life and less obsessive about always being right and looking perfect. Hmmm. I wonder whom she inherited those traits from? Her patience was most revealing when it came to teaching me the intricacies of cribbage. She didn't recount my cards, roll her eyes, and say "Duh!!!" She even listened to me more, perhaps because I wasn't harping at her to "Hurry up," as I had before.

Firmly settled into the routine, Zoë began to test me, as children do, when it came to the limits I set for her. She wanted to see how far I would extend my reach over her on Pelee Island. I had already conceded defeat (albeit privately) in the battle of hair bands. But I stuck to our regular routine of bedtimes, homework, and reading rather than watching TV.

When she asked to go for a walk by herself, I let her, though I sat by the large front window under the pretext of reading and surreptitiously watched where she went. It was a delight to see her hunched over a ditch trying to decipher the tiny insect life spawning as the winter ended. She picked out animal tracks and followed them. She pulled out her binoculars and trained them on a bird, eager to add a new species to the growing bird list she had taped to the fridge door when we first arrived.

I encouraged her outdoor freedom but some things I just couldn't sanction, such as night walks.

"But, Mom," Zoë complained, "who's going to kidnap me? We live on an island!"

I was worried not about a "who" but about a "what."

We still couldn't get over the darkness that enveloped us the moment the sun blazed its last rays for the day. I had never known a place that could go from day to night in such a short span of time. It was total blackness at night. Occasionally, to assure ourselves that it really was dark out there, and not just our imaginations, we would open the back door. It was as if a black sheet had been placed in front of our faces. We would dare each other to step outside. For all we knew, there was an endless abyss beyond the threshold.

As the weather warmed up, we got a bit braver and tested our faith that terra firma indeed lay beyond the kitchen door. Stumbling blindly for a few yards, we moved carefully and nervously away from the house before stopping and tilting back our heads to behold the night sky. Such a mass of stars! In the city, it has become more difficult to discern the stars from the streetlights: electric illumination has turned nighttime into just another shade of day. In our Pelee Island backyard, surrounded by true blackness, the effect was breathtaking. Zoë brought along her map of the night sky and flicked on her small flash-light. The sudden brightness hurt our eyes.

After a few minutes, I asked her to turn it off so that we could become part of the night's eerie stillness. She did, but when it was really dark and deathly quiet she flicked it on again and did her impersonation of *The Blair Witch Project*. That did it: I ordered her into the house with a sound scolding about scaring people, especially middle-aged women with nervous dispositions.

On the evenings we did go out, we always left the house by 5:00 p.m., when it was still light. When we returned in the blackness later, and realized we had forgotten to leave on the back-door light, it was almost impossible to find our way to the house from the driveway. At times, we had to put on the headlights of our car until one of us made it to the house and flicked on the porch light.

I think we remembered to leave the light on the night Zoë and I packed up a casserole and a plate of cornbread (I was an expert at making cornbread by now) and headed to the Legion (on a school night, no less) for the annual Crafty Ladies Potluck. I hadn't been going to the weekly craft nights, but no one seemed to hold it against me. Mary Lou was going, so was Gail. Franny had a guest at her B&B that night and was getting ready for a trip to Florida, so she wasn't going.

The details of such get-togethers were intentionally kept vague. A lack of detailed planning was part of the Pelee charm. In this case, it was Darith who had set the date, the time, and the place, and then launched a phone chain. When I received the invitation, I confessed to the caller that I wasn't a member of the craft league. That confession prompted a loud "So???"

So we went. It was the first week of March, and by this point everyone was suffering from cabin fever. As we assembled at the Legion, and someone flicked on the heat, I marvelled at how well and how easily women spring into action for such things. Woman after woman walked through the Legion's door balancing a huge bowl or pan or casserole dish of home-cooked food. When everything had been laid out and the lids of two dozen different dishes had been lifted, the aroma was unbelievable.

It was Lent, so I swore to myself for giving up desserts. I then remembered I had given up swearing for Lent. I always seem to choose ridiculous Lenten promises.

I kept looking toward the window to see if any of the island's menfolk were peering in, betting that women, in their boundless generosity, would take pity on the men and offer them a plateful. Not bloody likely here. More probable was that Darith would have taken a broom to all of them. She was the organizer, and this was ladies night.

We threw together a bunch of wobbly tables, topped them with blue tablecloths, set out the cutlery, paper napkins, and dinner plates. Then we lined up for the feast.

The hum of chatter heightened as we tucked into our dinner. Conversation wasn't restricted to the woman sitting next to you. It was nothing to have a conversation with a woman at a table on the other side of the room. There were no rules, no boundaries. When Michelle, Pelee's reserved and polite postmistress, went into the kitchen to get something, Darith hollered to her above the din that, since she was already in the kitchen, she could start the dishes. There was a sudden lull in the conversation just as Michelle mumbled her reply, "Kiss my ass." Of course, everyone heard it and almost fell out of their chairs with laughter.

Mary Lou sat next to me. She was a naturally gifted party girl: riotously funny, verbose, and exuding a constant stream of joie de vivre. Even her apparel managed to draw you in: a pin, a skirt, a necklace, earrings. You simply had to choose an item and her eyes would light up. "Well, let me tell you about this. It's the funniest story!"

Although Mary Lou and I had spent many hours together over the past several weeks, I discovered something about her she had never told me: she had been a nun — in a silent order, of all things. I almost choked on my food. If you ever meet Mary Lou, you'll know she is definitely not the silent type. She regaled me with some of her escapades, and I howled at the thought of her even being drawn to such a life.

She had entered the convent in her early 20s and left it a few years later — actually, she was thrown out — and then pursued a career in drama therapy, which she was practising on the island. She was married to Roger, they had three grown children, and in her spare time she ran the island's Art Works shop. I marvelled at how lucky we, on the outside of cloistered life, were to have people like Mary Lou stir things up, and what a crime it would have been to silence her considerable talents.

Sitting next to Mary Lou was Gail. Gail ran Twin Oaks B&B

with her husband, Jim (the Jim who had met Zoë and me at the airport on our first day). It turned out that Gail and I had worked at the same newspaper years ago, though we had never crossed paths. How strange it is, I thought, that the paths of people — sometimes the very people you work with — intersect later in life. Gail and Jim had just returned from Thailand, and she regaled us about their fascinating trip.

A few seats farther down was Amanda, who worked for the township. We all congratulated her on the spiffy new tourist brochures that had just been printed.

It was such a fine evening of camaraderie, void of the pretence that often permeates most all-women functions. There were no tiresome machinations, no insincere "How nice to see you" greetings, definitely no air-kissing.

We had all been asked to bring a wrapped gift worth five dollars for the present game. When your number was called, you picked a gift from the table or grabbed one that someone had already chosen. The object was to end up with the most coveted gift — in this case, it was an unwrapped item, a basket woven from grapevines by Janine. By a confluence of swappings and covert deals, Zoë was the last player, and she had her pick of the crop. Naturally, I gave her a look that said, "For God's sake, get that grapevine basket!" She did.

As people unwrapped their gifts, Gail failed to notice that the tissue paper from her gift had fallen onto a lit candle, and with a "whoosh" she found herself alternately juggling and batting away the flaming paper. Several of us sprang into action and stamped out the flames. There was a pause. And then another explosion of laughter. I was having some fun.

The next morning (amazingly, Zoë and I were able to get up early the morning after we had been out on a school night), I packed Zoë off to school and headed out on my regular walk. When I got back, there was a phone call from Franny. "What are you doing this morning?" she asked. "I have someone who really wants to meet you."

It turned out that her B&B guest was a professor from a Michigan university who was intrigued by my articles and by the subject of lifestyle sabbaticals.

I was hardly an expert in the area of such things — I only had my learner's permit. As I straightened up the living room before their arrival, I wondered what advice I should give or, indeed, whether I had any to give. Was there a magic key to a less chaotic lifestyle? Was I supposed to have it? If this guy was looking for sage advice, he had the wrong person. I didn't have sage in my kitchen, let alone in my spiritual arsenal.

When I met them at the door, Franny's guest — Marcus — was terribly polite and grateful that I had agreed to meet him. He must have thought women on retreats have busy schedules.

I invited him and Franny into the living room. I sat on the couch cross-legged, then quickly unfolded my legs because I thought it looked too Dalai Lama-ish. As I spoke, my hands inexplicably came together as if in prayer. They *never* do that! Eventually, I sat with one leg over the other and one of my hands tucked beneath my thigh. Franny poured tea.

There was an awkward silence. Marcus seemed to be struggling with what he wanted to say. So I asked him questions about what he did for a living. He was a scientist in the area of animal behaviour, particularly as it related to animal (and human) welfare and coping strategies. His team was discovering patterns in lab rats that had a disturbing correlation to human behavioural responses, particularly when the tests involved instilling confusion, which sent the aggression levels in the rats soaring.

As we spoke, Marcus gradually opened up, and it became clear he had something in common with his lab animals. He had built his own hamster wheel and couldn't get off it. He needed and wanted to take a few months to do exactly what I was doing, but he was afraid that by doing so he would ruin his chances for tenure. He also confided that a long-term relation-ship had slipped through his fingers because he was so relentlessly focused on his work.

"Well, isn't that the problem, then?" I said, figuring anyone could see that.

And Marcus could, but he still couldn't bring himself to commit to life instead of to a livelihood.

We spoke about the need for people to escape — to take leave of their routines in order to recharge, refocus, and make sure that what they're doing in life is consistent with what they want out of it. But therein lay the rub: people have trouble distinguishing between the two streams because society trans-mits so many mixed messages. As the messages become more intense, and people scramble to keep up, they become confused and disoriented. A corollary of this is that many are afraid to question certain messages for fear of being branded "stupid" or "behind the pack." It reminded me of a rather sinister line from *The Goblet of Fire* in which Mad-Eye Moody tells Harry Potter, "Decent people are so easy to manipulate." Indeed we are.

come on !?

Governments and corporations are the primary culprits, Marcus and I agreed. One day they espouse one position, and the following day they reverse it. Who can keep up? The media, too, are guilty. You read newspaper headlines about how bad the economy is, then turn the page and find another headline saying the economy is on an upswing. It's impossible to know who or what to believe. What's more, it's exhausting to figure it all out. It's easier to just give in and go along with the herd than to step out of line and raise your hand.

The same sense of confusion reigns in human relationships. We are taught that big decisions require deliberate, sober thought. However, it is the speed thinkers whom everyone admires. The measured thinkers are considered "not up to speed." No one seems to be concerned about reaching the correct decision, just the quick one.

That's where Marcus was: losing faith in a system he thought was manipulating him, yet afraid to cut the cord. I urged him to take some time off and think his life through before the regrets started piling up. What good is achieving tenure when your personal life is miserable? Besides, I added, life is a series of stops and starts: no one gets it right on the first go, and we aren't expected to. We need to start looking at life as a quilt made up of rich and colourful experiences rather than as a vicious end-game.

The next day, I was at the airport to pick up Ted, and I saw

Marcus preparing to board the plane back to the mainland. I wished him well and urged him not to be afraid to take a risk, especially one of his own design.

Ted was naturally inquisitive about this strange man I was hugging good-bye at the airport.

"Oh," I said, getting into the car, "he's just a scientist from Michigan who came over here to get some advice on life from me."

Ted closed his eyes and slowly shook his head, then threw his suitcase — and a few bags of groceries — into the back seat.

Chapter 13

PICKING UP THE PACE

Be still then, and know that I am God.
— Psalm 46:10

While January and February were quiet, there was a perceptible quickening of the pulse in March. It was as if everyone had been lounging on the couch for two months, and then — bam! — they remembered they had left something boiling on the stove.

The Pelee Project

Suddenly, there was actual traffic whizzing by my living room window. And I mean whizzing: with no posted speed limits on Pelee, East West Road was turning into the Molson Indy. Is there a fire? I wondered, peering out the window.

As I walked along South Shore Road, even Lake Erie looked busy. The ice floes that had formed like sculptures on the horizon had dissolved into a torrent of roiling waves that rammed the coastline with the force of a snow plough. The next day, the water had settled into such a smooth, still surface that it could have fooled a glazier.

The wildlife was also showing signs of a population explosion. The birds — robins, red-winged blackbirds, killdeers, bufflehead ducks — were returning to Pelee Island, the migratory gateway to Canada, and their spirited cacophony, which I heard in all its glory along South Shore Road, sounded like a roomful of opera singers practising an hour before curtain time.

As I was completing the final lap of my morning walk, I passed about five cars and trucks — that was high traffic in Pelee terms — and when Ed slowed down to say "Good morning" I asked him what the ruckus was about. "The ferry starts at the end of this week," he said. "We're all trying to get the island fixed up for the tourists. If you think this is bad, wait until the ferry actually starts running."

The place was bustling. It was like working at Disney World before the gates open. Even Irma's phone was ringing with tourists wanting to book rooms in her B&B. Dutifully, I quoted them the going rate and took their reservations.

The ferry, I learned, delineated the seasons on Pelee the way the solstice did in other cultures. Ferry season was the time when Pelee people made their living, and after a bleak winter the islanders, such as Ed, were itching for action. The hive of activity that erupted that week gave me a clear sense of just how important a ferry is to an island community.

It was also March Break for the school kids this week, and I wondered how I would keep Zoë amused. As luck would have it, Jim's two children from his previous marriage, Kaeleigh, eight, and Kieran, 10, were visiting from Windsor. They and Zoë became fast friends, and they were inseparable all week. I was thrilled. Zoë had spent so much time in adult company that I wondered whether she would be able to relate to people her own age. Kaeleigh and Kieran had the same sense of adventure as Zoë, and during the week — unusually balmy for March — they explored Pelee's coastline, forests, gullies, and streams. They lay on the ground and peered into pools of water as if they were peering through microscopes. They stomped into the house at lunch, discarding muddy boots and coats, wolfed down sandwiches, and went back outside to resume their expeditions. When they tired of their outdoor pursuits, they flopped on the living room floor and played the new Harry Potter board game that Mom had brought for Zoë a few weeks earlier. I had never seen children get along so well, especially children who couldn't choose their playmates. The days this carefree little trio spent together weren't long enough for them; they demanded, and were permitted, sleepovers. I thought they would tire of each other within days and that their friendship would be broken by some petty argument. It never happened, and I think it was because they were outdoors, enjoying a freedom most children in the West lack.

Sadly, many urbanites value technical adeptness over an awareness of nature. Some parents express pride that their child is glued to a computer screen for hours on end. "At least I know where he is," they say, justifying such behaviour. Watching Zoë and her friends play, I realized how unhealthy that attitude is: you're essentially holding a child hostage in a sunless room. You can still "know where he is" if you let your child outdoors. It's easier to do this in the country than in the city, where fast cars and shadowy characters threaten the lives of freedom-loving children, but if cities are so congested and dangerous, maybe they're not the best places to raise children.

Adam and Matt were also having March Break, but the logistics of getting them to Pelee for a few days were too difficult. Zoë and I would have to wait another month to see them. I spoke with the boys frequently on the phone. They wrote me letters and sent me tapes of their favourite music, songs they thought I would enjoy. I could tell from the tone of his letters and from his choice of music that Matt was still angry at me for choosing spiritual boot camp over him. I listened to his music, primarily songs by Eminem. I had brought a book of the rappers' lyrics with me, and I found myself captivated by both the cleverness of rap rhyme and so many apt expressions of the frustration and desperation inherent in modern life. After two days, I could recite *Slim Shady* better than most teens. Essentially, there isn't much difference between the angst of Eminem and that of middle-aged folks.

This March Break was certainly a change from previous ones. In other years, I had spent it in some tropical destination, taking one child with me in an annual rotation. The year before, I had accompanied my mom to Spain. This year I was definitely south — but not in the sense to which I was accustomed. While I was normally screaming for some tropical sunshine by March, this year I wasn't.

Instead, Zoë and I signed up for craft workshops and paczkis making at the Legion. I had never heard of paczkis before. According to Mary Lou, who led this particular baking orgy, paczkis are a Polish jam-filled doughnut made before Lent for Fat Tuesday. We were in the middle of Lent, but Pelee, I discovered, didn't always stick rigidly to the Julian calendar. I gamely stuck to my Lenten vow not to eat sweets, though the temptation was excruciating. Zoë, who had jam and pastry flour smeared over her mouth, but didn't seem to be concerned about it, took to the assembly line production easily, keeping pace and giggling with Kaeleigh.

When we got home later that evening, I told Zoë she should wash her face well to get all the baking ingredients off it. "What ingredients?" she asked, truly perplexed. She ran into the washroom and, looking at herself in the mirror, let out a scream followed by, "WHY DIDN'T YOU TELL ME!!!"

The next day, Zoë headed back to the Legion with Kaeleigh and Kieran for crafts and a movie, and Mary Lou popped in for tea. Mary Lou and I had developed a habit of checking in with each other weekly, even daily, on how we were faring on our respective spiritual journeys. She and other islanders with whom I was comfortable speaking about these matters knew such a journey didn't come with an estimated time of arrival: it was a long, ponderous, and sometimes onerous trek. The beauty was that it was the type of journey that forced you to take your time and enjoy the scenery along the way.

I was so grateful to have Mary Lou around to talk to about my beliefs. Many of my urban friends tensed up whenever I mentioned the G word. I had begun to tune in to God — really tune in to God — a few weeks after decompressing from urban life. My bond with God was strengthening to the point where I vowed nothing and no one would pull me away from it. I had taken God off my linear to-do list and firmly planted Him at the centre of my new life. Now, I told Mary Lou, I woke up each morning and mentally pictured God at the centre of my personal circle and allowed my myriad worries, chores, activities, and responsibilities to float freely around Him. That way I remained focused on the central purpose of my life rather than on the transient flotsam and jetsam that infiltrate human life. After decades of making lists, this was indeed a shift for me.

I explained to Mary Lou that I continued to be inspired by everyone I met, and I was convinced that God put us all in each other's path, for better or for worse, to learn something from the experience. But I was also beginning to comprehend that it was through our failures and our frailties — not our perfections and successes — that we connected with people.

I was also tapping into a spiritual energy, particularly during my walk, and I told Mary Lou about an odd experience

I'd had that morning: I was walking up Stone Road when a slight breeze arose, and, although there were many dead leaves on the road, only one moved, and it moved noisily in a beeline toward me. I looked at it, and it stopped short of my feet. Why didn't the other leaves move? There was nothing holding them in place. I kept walking, and a dozen or so paces ahead I turned around. The leaf that had moved toward me was fixed where it had stopped at my feet. Suddenly a breeze picked up. The leaf remained unmoved while the other leaves came to life and swirled around it. I stood and watched, but still my leaf didn't budge.

"What do you suppose that was all about?" I asked Mary Lou as I prepared our afternoon tea.

"There are dozens of tiny miracles that occur daily, but we're never open to them," she said. "We're either too busy or too cynical to pay them any attention."

Which led me to wonder: when is one mind deemed "open to experience" and another mind deemed "delusional"?

Before we knew it, it was almost 4:30, the time I had promised to pick up Zoë, Kaeleigh, and Kieran from the Legion.

When Zoë and I returned home, it was time to head to Dan's for dinner. Dan was having a bunch of people in and had invited us. In addition to writing, laundry, cooking, and cleaning, socializing was taking up a good and welcome portion of my calendar. I had a lot of news to deliver to Dan's dinner party.

My Hamilton house sold this week, and the sale brought both relief and grief. It sold on the fifth anniversary of the date I had originally purchased it. As much as I loved our home, I knew it was time to move on. It had sustained my little family and helped us to grow through a period of tumultuous change, and now, I figured, we were entering yet another transitional period.

I had no idea where this new period would lead us, but at that moment it was of no consequence. I was still in love with my Pelee life, and I didn't want it to end. A few of my Pelee friends had suggested I apply for a job on the ferry, and the thought was tempting. But as much as I wanted my freedom, I had a responsibility to return to my children. I could see no way around it.

I explained this over dinner at Dan's. His niece, Judy, had become another of my Pelee pals, flying in on occasion from her home in Cleveland to keep Dan company and to check up on the renovations being done to her own cottage. Dick was also there — Dan's home seemed to be Dick's second home. I couldn't imagine leaving these people behind. They genuinely hoped I would stay, but they understood my reasons for having to leave. Still, I told them, I was weeks away from my departure date, and who knew what was around the corner.

Immediately around my corner was a visit with Ted in Windsor the next day, my first visit to the mainland in two months. Zoë's father was arriving to spend the weekend with Zoë on Pelee, and since there wasn't enough room on the island for both of us, I booked passage for Zoë, me, and our car on the morning ferry. Zoë would meet her dad on the Leamington dock and travel back with him to Pelee. I tucked her into bed that night. She was squirming with excitement about seeing her father.

We were therefore unprepared for the sight that greeted us the following morning. After several balmy days, days warm enough to coax the crocuses out of hibernation, we awoke to the wind howling at such a rate we feared our home would be lifted off the ground. When we raised the window blinds, we couldn't see across the road: a blizzard was roaring, and it had already dumped a foot of snow on the ground.

I quickly called Zoë's dad in Hamilton and warned him of the weather and of the chance — a good chance, it seemed — that the ferry would be cancelled. He said it was snowing where he was too, but he was determined to make the trip.

My next call was to George. He had offered to hose down my muddy car before I took it to the mainland. Audrey answered the phone. I explained that, given the weather, the car wash was off. When I mentioned to her that we were booked on the ferry, she said her son, Dave, would be at the helm.

"Won't the voyage be cancelled because of this weather?" I asked.

"Not with Dave steering it," Audrey said with motherly determination. "If it's bad, he'll cancel. But he has good instincts about this. You'll get to the mainland safely."

Next I called Bev, a small claims court judge from London, Ontario, who owned a number of properties on Pelee Island. We had met the night before at Dan's house and she had offered to show us her collection of houses the next morning. I figured our outing would be cancelled.

But Bev was insistent. "It's only a bit of snow," she said. "I'll see you here at 9:30."

Only a bit of snow? Was she crazy? I turned to Zoë. "We're going out to look at houses," I said.

"In this weather?" she asked incredulously. Even she knew a bad storm when she saw it.

We bundled up and headed outside. The back door almost blew off its hinges, and we swung around and struggled to hold it down while I fumbled with a hook that would secure it in place.

In the car, we sat shivering in our seats as the engine warmed up, the force of the wind rocking our car. Then we set off tentatively, stunned that we had ventured out in such weather for the sake of a house tour. The roads were so clogged with snow that I feared we would get stuck. Several times I considered returning home.

We eventually made it to Bev's home, located at the far northeast corner of the island. It was the first of four homes she was going to show us. We pulled into her driveway, got out of the car with difficulty, and put our shoulders to the wind as we staggered to her front door.

Once inside, we plopped down on her couch, windwhipped. I looked out her windows to an awesome view of the lake, and watched the waves smash the beach and the breakwater. I turned around and wondered what Bev had in her cigarette that would make her call this "a bit of snow." We wandered around her home, trying to thaw out. It was lovely: panoramic views of the lake, modern facilities, pine antiques, a video library that rivalled those of some stores I had been in, and a huge stone fireplace.

"If I knew you were looking for a place to stay over the winter, you could have stayed here," she said.

Now she tells me, I thought. But as gorgeous as her home was, it would have been too opulent for the purpose of my retreat. I needed simpler surroundings. I thanked her and told her I would take her up on her offer if and when I needed another retreat.

We ventured out into the storm, which seemed to be picking up strength by the minute. Bev jumped into her red Saab, and Zoë and I followed obediently in our car as we went from house to house.

One house I had a particular interest in was the stone Regency cottage built by Alexander McCormick in 1847. I detected ghosts the moment I walked in, but I loved it regardless. I tried to imagine the life that had taken place within these walls so long ago and what Pelee must have been like at that time.

I *tried* to do this, but I couldn't. We were distracted by the howling wind, and our concern was mounting for Zoë's dad to get safely to Leamington. As much as he and I had battled over the years, I realized how distraught I would be if something happened to him.

We thanked Bev for the tour; rather, we screamed ourselves hoarse above the storm saying thanks, and told her we had to go because we were booked on the noon ferry.

"In this weather?" she asked. "Are you crazy?"

Sheesh.

When we got back to the house, the phone was ringing. It was Dan. He lived on the east side of the island, the same side Bev did.

"Darlin'," he said in his American drawl, "you're not goin' on the ferry today."

"It's been cancelled?" I asked.

"Well, I don't know about that; I'm just tellin' you, you're not goin'. The waves here are terrible. It's not worth risking your life."

"But I have a hair appointment in Leamington," I said jokingly, though I really did have a hair appointment in Leamington.

"No, don't go, darlin'. Stay where you are."

I hung up.

The phone rang again. This time it was Dick. He lived on the west side of the island, and he delivered his report. "I've only seen it worse than this back in . . . ," he said, regaling me about a previous storm that had been so bad he had become queasy onboard, which was uncommon for him, he said.

I told him Audrey had said her son, Dave, was at the helm and sailing regardless of the storm.

"He is?" said Dick. "Well, that's why he's known around here as Make-'em-Heave Dave. Don't go, Jane. It's bad out there, as bad as they come."

I considered both these caring phone calls. I faced a dilemma. What to do? I called Ted.

"It's snowing here, but it's not bad," he reported from Windsor.

Zoë and I got into the car and headed for the West Dock. Sure enough, passengers and cars were boarding the plucky *Pelee Islander*.

As I waited at the ticket gate, lights flashed behind me. It was Judy. I was supposed to meet her at the Legion for the weekly Friday lunch. I got out of the car and went over to talk to her. We had to yell at each other to hear ourselves above the noise of the storm. She told me she was flying back to Cleveland that afternoon.

"That's really brave," I hollered. "But shouldn't you wait it out another day?"

"I can't," she yelled back. "I've got a hair appointment."

"Me too!" I laughed.

Nothing, it seemed, kept women from their hair appointments.

Zoë and I drove onto the *Pelee Islander* and huddled together in the lounge. The waves were rocking us fiercely, and I hardly noticed when we pulled away from the dock. We were thrown about like airline luggage, and I thought I was going to be sick. Zoë, meanwhile, loved it, saying it was like a roller coaster.

I was worried about what we would find on the other side. Would her dad make it on time? What if he had an accident? How would we find out?

Amazingly, I made it across the lake without tossing my cookies. I didn't see Captain Dave, but I'm sure he didn't once take his strong hands off the wheel or his eyes off the water.

Zoë and I drove off the ferry and then waited tensely in the parking lot. I kept her spirits up by singing songs along with the radio, but we were both worried. It was a long wait. Suddenly, her dad's car sped into the parking lot. We both jumped out of the car and raced to hug him. Then I remembered we were divorced and I wasn't supposed to do that anymore. I told him, instead, that we had been worried, but he was so excited to see Zoë he hardly noticed my blubbering. I waved good-bye and took off to my hair appointment.

The storm followed me all the way, and my newly coiffed hair was drenched by the time I had walked from the salon to my car at the curb. I wondered how Judy was faring with her appointment.

I drove on to Windsor, anxious to get out of the storm and into a big glass of wine and dinner at a restaurant. I was really looking forward to spending a day or so in the city, but once I was there everything seemed so vast and sterile, including the newly opened Windsor Art Gallery. Nothing made me feel cosy and warm. Instead, I retreated to Ted's tiny apartment and suggested we just stay in.

On Sunday morning, I headed back to Leamington. I met Zoë at the dock. Apparently, the return voyage to Pelee that frightful Friday had been as smooth as glass. They had spent the weekend exploring the island together. Her dad studied me carefully and said, "But I don't know how you, of all people, can stand it out there. Even I'd go crazy."

I told him I loved it so much that I would live there in a heartbeat if I had the money.

He shook his head in disbelief. This was definitely not the Jane he remembered.

Chapter 14

THE LAND WHERE
PEOPLE DON'T WAVE

Now I see the secret of the making of the best persons.
It is to grow in the open air and to eat and sleep with the earth.
— Walt Whitman

Not only wasn't I the Jane my ex-husband remembered, but I wasn't even the Jane *I* remembered. And good riddance to her too.

March Break was over. Pelee shifted into high gear for its

tourist season, and Zoë headed back to school. Now the islanders were busy, and I wasn't. While such idleness would once have made me feel guilty amid the swirl of such activity, it didn't faze me. I kept walking and watching and enjoying my solitude. Zoë and I had a month left on our Pelee retreat, and I was determined to wring every last drop from it.

Since the ferry service had resumed, traffic on the island was heavier. Trucks were hauling building supplies for cottage renovations, and linen and food supplies for the hotel and B&Bs. I could tell by the traffic when the ferry had docked; in fact, I could almost set my watch to the precise moment when I would hear the rumble of trucks tearing down East West Road to some construction site. I could also tell the foreigners from the islanders — they didn't wave, even when you waved to them first. "Damn mainlanders," I muttered derisively.

Spring had sprung again. The previous week's dumping of snow had melted along with the memory of it. Trees resumed their budding, and crocuses dizzily straightened their storm-battered stems, dusted off the snow, and craned their wobbly necks toward the sun. The landscape began to green rapidly. As I stared at it, I saw how conducive Pelee's barren landscape was to soul rejuvenation. There wasn't a speck of distraction anywhere: not a brightly coloured flower, not a pretty meadow, not a meandering, babbling river. It was stark, it was plain, it was flat, it was beige. It was, I decided, perfect.

When your surroundings are stripped bare, the physical world is so transparent. Leafy branches or flowering shrubs tend to impede your view of what lies beyond. It works the same way with people: when you strip humans of their techno-gizmos, fancy clothes, and fast talk, it's easier to find their core personalities. You aren't distracted by their flash and glitter. Even when we look at ourselves in the mirror, we can easily be distracted by an earring, a blemish, a brightly coloured scarf. I now congratulated myself on having packed the perfect wardrobe for this adventure. It was serviceable and without a smidgen of distraction. Like the landscape, I had become transparent. On Pelee Island, I didn't seem so complicated, and my life didn't seem so chaotic.

The past few months of rural life had opened my eyes to the beauty of nature, and now I was humbled by it. As I took my morning constitutional, I found beauty in what many might dismiss as banal. Gee, maybe I'll even try camping, I thought. The idea was barely in my mind when I imagined breaking the news to my city friends: many of them camped, but none dared to put the words *camp* (at least in the outdoorsy sense) and *Jane* in the same sentence. The vision of me at a campsite would probably make them spew out their coffee in mid-gulp. To them, I was the gal whose idea of roughing it meant staying at a Holiday Inn. But 70-plus days in the wilderness had allowed me to shed some inhibitions and undo some of the typecasting I had inadvertently inflicted on myself, and for which I was wholly responsible. Now I was ready to challenge every stereotype anyone had affixed to me. Yes, I was still a square peg in a round world, but, in the wise words of Mary Lou, "Sooooo?" So, indeed.

My friend Dan, too, had imparted some wise words to me:

"Should'ves, could'ves, and would'ves don't count for anything, darlin'." He was right; the past was past. There wasn't even any point in deconstructing it. Accept your lessons, admit you screwed up (or didn't), and move forward.

It was time for Zoë and me to test our rural sensitivities against the urban jungle. Ted had managed to get a pair of tickets to a Joe Jackson concert in Detroit, so we timed our trip to Windsor accordingly. This would be Zoë's first trip off the island since she had arrived three months earlier, and I was eager to see how she would react to city life. Thus, we boarded the *Pelee Islander* on Wednesday morning and sailed to the Land Where People Don't Wave. We landed in Leamington and began our gradual descent into urban society.

I stifled a chuckle as Zoë reflexively raised her hand to wave at the oncoming cars and withdrew it with sudden embarrassment when she realized her mistake. But she was almost hostile when we sat at a traffic light for a minute. We hadn't had to stop at a light for months — there weren't any on Pelee Island. Her eyes widened as we passed row upon row of billboards, traffic signs, malls, cars, jaywalking pedestrians, enormous trucks blasting their horns, fast-food joints as far as the eye could see — and we were only in Leamington. Everything was larger than life. From SUVs to transport trucks to buildings — the world looked huge, ugly, and menacing, and we could feel ourselves recoil and cower.

As we neared Windsor, the signs became more brash, the trucks larger, the motels seedier, the fast-food joints more plentiful. We had no idea it was Roll-Up-the-Rim time in Canada. The terrain was one congested mass of confusing directional signs, marquees, and billboards.

We spotted a car wash and pulled in. Our car had been coated in Pelee mud for so long we had forgotten its true colour — in fact, after it was washed, we had trouble finding it in parking lots over the next few days.

The Ambassador Bridge linking Windsor with Detroit loomed in front of us. Zoë and I compared the cities' competing skylines and decided both had a lot to answer for.

We drove to Ted's place, dropped our bags, and announced we wanted to go to the mall. Ted reluctantly agreed. Once there, Zoë and I were helpless. Everything was so garish and so crass that it held us spellbound. It was like passing an accident: you couldn't help looking at the wreckage even though you really just wanted to turn away. In food courts, we watched as people stared into space and stuffed greasy confections into their mouths. Their stomachs were full, but their eyes looked empty. We stared at the clothing artfully displayed in the store windows. Everything we liked, it turned out, was men's wear — great, baggy clothes. The women's clothing looked as tight and flimsy as Saran Wrap. Was this our millennium's version of Japanese foot binding?

That night Ted and I went into Detroit for the Joe Jackson concert. The concert was terrific, and it was great to be out with Ted, but I found myself missing Zoë terribly. Except for the one weekend she had spent with her father, we hadn't been apart in months; everywhere I had gone, she had gone. I declined Ted's offer of a drink after the show; I wanted to see my daughter.

The next day, desperate to buy at least one item of clothing on this trip, Zoë and I decided to check out Value Village, a chain of secondhand clothing stores. Two hours later, we emerged with a ton of great stuff for under $70. I found a Christian bookstore and bought a copy of the *Spiritual Renewal Bible*, the same version Shawn and Melissa had lent me a few weeks earlier.

But what Zoë and I saved on clothing we lost on other things. I learned a new lesson: fast food is the scourge of diets and pocketbooks. I made a tactical error by taking Zoë to a matinee on an empty stomach. The theatre was located in an industrial mall removed from even the suburbs. We were stranded, hungry captives. Two movie tickets, mini pizzas slathered in gooey cheese, and a vat of pop totalled $30. Yikes! What's more, neither of us had touched this kind of food in months.

By the end of three days, Zoë had a cold and a raft of pimples, and I had enough gas to fuel a space shuttle. I marginally managed to redeem myself with a game of squash and a dip in the whirlpool at Ted's fitness club. It seemed like luxury.

As kind and hospitable as Ted was, we couldn't wait to leave. City life was making us sick, and we missed our island. Zoë and I got up early the next day and loaded the car for the trip back to Pelee.

When we arrived at Leamington's dock, we discovered the voyage had been cancelled because of severe winds. It was half as bad as the storm the week before, but of course no one could remember that. It was 10 a.m., and the next ferry wasn't leaving until 6 p.m. Damn. We were exhausted, dirty, and on the verge of contracting scurvy.

As a diversion, we headed for Colasanti's, a garden centre-cum-family playground located outside Leamington. We could while away the hours there, I suggested. We petted the animals and played mini golf. Then we had lunch, and the sight of Zoë's huge plate of onion rings almost made me heave. Even scarier was the fact that she didn't really want them; they had just seemed like the thing to order.

We returned to the car. It was freezing outside. We still had five hours to kill (time goes so slowly when you don't want it to), so we drove around looking for a Tim Hortons, hoping a coffee would help me to stay awake. I felt slovenly, and I looked like I had been on a one-week bender.

With so much time before the ferry left, Zoë and I decided to drive the 45 minutes back to Windsor. We ended up at Wendy's. Thankfully, Wendy's sold baked potatoes, just plain baked potatoes. My body was craving unadorned, ungreasy food.

I found a payphone and called the Leamington dock. The familiar voice of Patti, who worked at the Pelee terminal, came on the line. I didn't know Patti that well, but at that moment she was like a family member to me because we shared an island for a home. She assured me that the ferry was running and that we were booked on the next passage. Zoë and I jumped in the car, and drove like the blazes to Leamington again.

The *Pelee Islander* was loading its cargo and passengers when we arrived. The winds were still strong, but the crew felt confident the little boat could make the journey.

It was a turbulent trip, but the intrepid *Pelee Islander* persevered as the sky darkened. Waves crashed against the windows, and we were rocked by the swells. But we weren't scared. We were going home.

Someone switched on the TV in the boat's lounge, and a hockey game came in clear and bright. Was there a more quintessential Canadian moment than this: sitting in an old ferry in the middle of the Great Lakes watching *Hockey Night in Canada*?

Zoë peered out the window to see if she could make out Pelee Island in the distance. "Mom, come and see," she said excitedly. "It looks like New York out there. Seriously!"

I staggered across the boat and looked out the window. There were indeed lights, about two dozen, that marked the island's West Dock. I chuckled at her innocent comparison. It was probably the first time Pelee Island had been mistaken for the Big Apple.

We drove off the ferry, and both of us let out a sigh. I think it was the first time I had exhaled in three days. Into the darkness we travelled, down the unlit roads. We passed a car, and its driver honked a greeting to us. We were finally back in the Land Where People Wave.

Chapter 15

INTO THE CLASSROOM

Education is an admirable thing, but it is well to remember from time to time that nothing that is worth knowing can be taught.
— *Oscar Wilde*

I awoke Monday morning with my daughter standing over me, a look of panic on her face.

The Pelee Project

Her class had begun a unit on newspapers, and I had volunteered whatever expertise I could to her teacher, Mrs. N. My job was to instruct the grades-six-to-eight class on the fine art of looking at a newspaper critically, and on writing for one.

Now Zoë was reciting a strict list of things I mustn't do in her classroom that might cause her embarrassment — such as showing up. I promised not to call her "pumpkin," not to scold the two boys who were forever getting into mischief, not to giggle, not to assign homework. Kathie, my pal at the *Post*, had shipped me a boxful of teaching materials as well as *National Post* notepads and pencils. Branding was big.

I drove to the West Dock that morning and purchased 15 copies of the day's newspaper, thereby sending the *Post's* single-copy sales through the roof that day and, quite possibly, causing a frisson of excitement among the executive ranks as they noted that more than 15 — 15! — newspapers were now being purchased on Pelee Island. I could just imagine the boardroom conversation: "Peterson! Where is that place again? Get Reader Sales and Service on the line immediately, and tell them to get moving on a subscription blitz!"

As I handed out the newspapers to the students, I considered my opening remarks: "OK, kids, can you say 'right-wing agenda'?" They weren't the most media-savvy group. Some admitted, a little too proudly I thought, that their families didn't read newspapers: they got their news from U.S. television stations. One student even said that all the news his family cared to read was contained in the *Grapevine*, the six-page mimeographed collection of ads, birthday announcements, and

Legion lunch menus that was circulated among the islanders.

I tried to show the students examples of biased writing, but first I had to define the word *bias*. When I asked them to compare two stories on the same subject, one smart cookie pointed out that both basically expressed the same point of view — they just used different words. I punished her impudent outburst by making her read Andrew Coyne.

I wanted to rhapsodize about the cynical humour of Mark Steyn, the token nod to left-wing politics in Linda McQuaig's infrequent column that was always buried on page 598 in the business section, the way the *Post* always stuck a picture of a babe on the front page. But in the end, I showed them where to find the comics (the *Post* ran comics once upon a time), the horoscopes, and sports.

My 45-minute teaching stint was proclaimed a success by Zoë, though I had committed the cardinal sin of assigning homework. The notepads and pencils had been a clear hit, she reported.

I returned to the classroom the next day, horrified to discover that the students hadn't done the homework I had assigned. I looked around the classroom for the strap. Mrs. N. gamely shrugged her shoulders.

I returned again a few days later. This time some of the homework had been done, and the students were busy putting together their own newspaper. Their assignment was to seek out pertinent news from their island to include in it.

One piece of news unlikely to make it into the school newspaper concerned Al, Pelee's bon vivant reeve, who also happened to be the manager of the island's liquor store. It was discovered he had used his store as a sort of after-hours club for his buddies during the bleak winter nights. He was relieved of his managerial duties but continued on as reeve. There was no police officer on the island, so it was surmised that one of the islanders had snitched on him. Of course, news of this sort was never found in the *Grapevine*: you actually had to hear it through the other grapevine.

While an incident like that on the mainland would have been scandalous, many of the islanders seemed to look the other way; a few even excused the reeve's behaviour. I was confused by their reaction. Weren't laws laws?

With mere weeks left until the end of our retreat, I looked around for places I hadn't visited and people I hadn't spent enough time with. One of these people was Zane. Zane had a gruff demeanour that sometimes scared people away. Always up to a challenge and undaunted by curmudgeons — there were already plenty of them in my life — I phoned up Zane. He had been on the island forever and done everything on it, from running the ferry service to owning the grocery store to serving as township reeve. He had done it all; he had seen it all. What's more, he loved the island. Maybe a little too much. Rumour had it that when his second wife could no longer hack island life and presented an it's-the-island-or-me ultimatum, Zane calmly pulled the ferry schedule out of his back pocket and told her when the next boat was leaving.

Zane was part of the island's royalty, having descended from the McCormicks. (I gradually learned that I was about the only person on the island not related to the McCormicks in some way.) He rarely came out to social functions and was a bit reclusive. He went about his business, tapping Franny's maple trees for sap or keeping an eye on her place when Franny was off the island, taking in the islanders' discarded pop cans for recycling, creating amazing things out of wood, and fixing up the grounds of the Pelee Island Sportsman's Club.

Zane had been burned a few times by the islanders, and when you sat him down he eventually, albeit carefully, spilled the beans. What you also discovered was his wealth of island lore, his kind heart, and his rebel spirit. He was easy to be around, and since he loved talking, and I had learned to love listening, we were a good match. He settled himself at my dining room table with a mug of tea.

I hadn't managed to get out trap shooting with Sondi, but I was still keen on learning. Since Zane was a past president of the Sportsman's Club, I told him I was interested in joining. He was surprised but took my money and issued me a membership card. Apart from an ignominious stint as a Girl Guide, this was about the only club I had ever joined.

Our conversation drifted from guns to history to women's lib; Zane didn't buy into women's lib, saying he was suspicious of a woman who didn't take her husband's surname. And he didn't like double-barrelled surnames either. When I pointed out that his own mother had joined her maiden name with her married one, he chuckled. "You got me there," he said.

The Pelee Project

Marion McCormick Hooper, a formidable woman in her own right, had written a blistering but highly entertaining and comprehensive history of Pelee Island as her personal centennial project in 1967. *Pelee Island: Then and Now* had ruffled more than a few feathers, Zane admitted, but he admired his mother's ability to stand her ground.

Our visit ended too soon, but as he was leaving Zane told me he had enjoyed my columns. He said that it was fun having me on the island, that I had "shaken things up." He didn't come out and say he would miss me, but he asked me to keep in touch. And he promised to lend me his mother's book, as long as I promised to return it. I did read the book — it was a remarkable piece of work — and after I returned Zane's copy I purchased my own.

During our chat, Zane had talked about the pheasant hunts, how important they were to the island's economy, and how gun control issues were sounding the death knell of Pelee's bread and butter. His remarks about hunting prompted me to pay a visit the next day to the pheasant farm.

When I arrived, Shayne, who managed the Pelee Island Pheasant Farm, was in his office attending to the sorts of details that naturally precede the arrival of 10,000 chicks. He and his small crew were prepping the pens, clearing the water lines, and doing minor repairs.

Pheasants aren't docile creatures, as I had learned a few weeks earlier. I was driving down Henderson Road and ran into a pheasant — though not hard enough, as it turned out. Catching sight of him, I slowed down to admire his plumage

— the male of the species is extraordinarily beautiful — when he darted out in front of my car. I slammed on my brakes and held my breath. Had I hit him? Then his little head emerged from under my car, and he began squawking at me with such anger that he frightened me. I didn't know whether to ignore him or back up and run over him. I decided to drive on, but he took chase, screaming at me and pecking at my tires. Later that night, when I surveyed my dwindling bank account, I wondered whether I should have mowed him down. There were at least two good meals and a casserole in that bird.

I mentioned the incident to Shayne. This particular pheasant had terrorized a number of islanders, and its antics had been reported in *The Windsor Star*. Shayne muttered something about someone having taken care of the situation.

He showed me the pens and talked about the extreme vigilance necessary to keep the flock alive until the hunt. If other animals or birds didn't invade the pens and gobble them up, the pheasants could just as easily prey on their own. They were prone to cannibalism.

The weather had warmed up considerably. It had been an early and quick spring. The bitter wind had muted to a soft, sweet-smelling breeze, and the islanders were predicting a long, hot summer, which would bode well for the tourist trade.

Meanwhile, the date for our departure loomed. Reluctantly and sadly, I began winding down our tour of duty. While we packed up some boxes and took stock of what was left in the fridge, I also took stock of myself.

The previous week's excursion to Windsor had opened my eyes to how much both Zoë and I had changed. Now I could feel my body tense as I made plans for our return to urban life. I felt so unaffected and carefree on the island, and the prospect of city life terrified me. How could I even begin to shine amid the many diversions and distractions of a city? I worried about getting sucked back into the cyclone of activity. I began questioning whether I had what it took to stay rooted to the attitudes and insights I had imprinted on my psyche since arriving on Pelee Island. Would I indeed prove my mother right and fall into my old habits once I stood at the corner of Bloor and Yonge streets?

The time I had spent these past three months had given me the luxury to filter and reflect on my behaviour. I had stepped back from the fray and observed society not from an ivory tower but at eye level regarding how and where I fit in. I worried that the pace of modern life beyond Pelee Island would throw me off my practised stride. Yet I was sure I could withstand the temptations and soldier through the urban minefield: I had met some spectacular bimbos in my urban life, and they managed to survive very well. If I couldn't handle it, then what did that say about me?

In an attempt to acclimatize myself to the fast lane, I turned on the TV one morning. The *Today* show was on, and one of its hosts, Matt Lauer, was interviewing a lawyer with such rapid-fire questions and without any concern for his guest's comfort that I almost jumped to my feet and shouted "Your honour, the host is clearly badgering the guest!" After two minutes, I flicked the TV off. It was one of the few times I had sympathy for a lawyer.

When did we stop listening to one another? Why did we have to steamroller our way over others in a constant bid for oneupmanship? Interrupting the conversations of others was a crime I had been guilty of numerous times, and perhaps the reason I turned off the TV so quickly was because I was staring a bad habit in the face. I saw a bit of myself in Lauer's lack of grace.

The sad fact of urban life is that, as the pace quickens, the number of social courtesies declines exponentially. Resisting the urban pace and maintaining a civilized demeanour are more work than many of us can handle. It becomes too easy to slip into a morass of fast talk, rapid-fire comebacks, and sharp witticisms. In our culture, the faster you speak and the quicker you reply, the more brilliant you are deemed.

A few islanders were forthright about my metamorphosis since arriving on their shores. To be fair, they had known me only a few months, but all of them, to a man (and a woman), agreed I no longer moved like a poodle on amphetamines. They also said I talked more slowly, gestured less, and was more reflective.

It was the comment about my slower speech that particularly resonated with me. I found that, when I slowed down my speech, I could slow down my world and make everything less urgent. I noticed I answered the phone more slowly. Mere months ago, I would pick up the receiver with an abrupt "H'lo?" I now sounded out each syllable — "Hel-lo?" — or even said "Good morning."

The Pelee Project

I don't know why we are all so afraid to slow down. We have elevated busyness to a golden attribute. If people hear urgency in our voices, they know we are busy and hence important. Slow speech conveys laziness and mental impairment. Speak slowly to someone, and you'll detect a hint of impatience in his or her demeanour because you are deliberately forcing that person to slow down.

I experienced this when I called my editor at the *Post* this week. Dianne and I normally communicated by e-mail, but occasionally we spoke by phone. She is a fast speaker, and by the middle of March I couldn't understand a word she said. When I asked her to repeat what she had said, I could picture her sticking pins in her eyes at her desk as she slowly sounded out every syllable for me as if I was brain damaged.

Dianne wasn't the only speed talker. I called my friend Kathie. She kept putting me on hold to answer the hundreds of calls she gets in her job each day. I knew she was busy, so it didn't matter to me, but when she put me on hold the telephone line automatically defaulted to a local radio station. The traffic report came on, and, as I gazed out my Pelee window at the empty landscape, I listened to the same litany of problems I had heard three months before: "Bumper to bumper both ways on the Don Valley Parkway . . . slow across the top of the city, especially approaching Pearson airport. . . ." I muttered a prayer of thanks that I wasn't anywhere near it. The rapid-fire delivery of the reporters left me incredulous that anyone short of a linguistic expert could comprehend them.

It reminded me of a rather amusing incident that happened

to me several months before I left for Pelee Island. As a long-distance commuter, I relied on a particular station's frequent traffic reports to get a bead on what was happening ahead of me on my route. One evening, as I was heading home, I listened intently to the traffic report on my car radio. But the reporter, communicating from an aircraft high above the city, spoke so fast I couldn't follow what he said. It was bad enough that people spoke quickly to each other, but when radio announcers spoke faster than what the general population could comprehend things were really out of whack. Furious, I grabbed my cellphone and phoned the radio station to complain. The traffic reporter himself picked up the call. "Can I help you?" he asked.

Stammering from a mixture of surprise, intimidation, and anger, I blurted: "You spoke too fast. I'm on my way home, and I have no idea what route to take."

He laughed, perhaps embarrassed, perhaps mocking me, I don't know. He asked where exactly I was on the road and then kindly told me the precise route that would get me home quickly.

Now, as I waited on hold, the traffic report shifted to the news. It was delivered so quickly that the announcers were tripping over their own words. Ugh! How would I ever adjust to that life again? Like Scarlett O'Hara, I decided not to think about it today; I would think about it tomorrow. Besides, I was expecting company: Ted and his young son, Michael, were arriving for the weekend, and so was Irma, newly returned from her southern holiday. There was a big shindig at the Legion that weekend — the Hillbilly Hoedown — and when Irma caught wind of it she asked if she could come out and stay overnight.

What could I say? It was her house.

It was great to see her again, and I knew at once how she felt about being back on the island. If I had trouble being away from Pelee for a day or two, how did she feel being away for nearly four months? Even though she had spent most of her holiday in Florida — warm weather, lots of sunshine — she said she had missed the island constantly.

She walked into her home and looked pleased. I hadn't wrecked anything. She looked at the plants and gasped. "You must have a green thumb," she marvelled. "Look at how they've grown!"

They had, and all I had done was water them. No house-plant had ever survived under my watch before. Weekly watering obviously works, I thought.

If Irma had any doubts that the islanders had forgotten about her, those doubts vanished the moment she walked into the Legion that night in her cowboy finery. She received so many welcome-home hugs that she must have felt like a million bucks.

It was a hilarious evening. It seemed the entire island population was in attendance. Young and old were dressed up and in high spirits. The children strutted around in their cowboy hats, blowing their toy whistles. I marvelled again at how such a diverse group of people could be bound together. Despite the dwindling population, I hoped they would all keep the faith and keep their island community strong. I hoped that some of the children I saw running through the Legion wouldn't be lured by distant lights, and would raise their own families on Pelee.

Chapter 16

THE SEWAGE HITS
THE VENTILATION SYSTEM

To contrive a little kingdom, in the midst of the universal muck,
then shit on it, ah that was me all over.
— Samuel Beckett

It was Monday and our penultimate week on Pelee Island. Ted
had extended his visit with us so he could play teacher at PIPS. I
had generously volunteered his talents to Mrs. N. for the

newspaper unit when the topic turned to news photography. Ted is an award-winning shooter, and I knew the students would learn a lot from him. Given the choice between looking at pictures and decoding neocon agendas, the kids would prefer the pictures, I figured.

While Ted grudgingly performed his duty — "Don't *ever* volunteer me for anything again!" were his last words as I delivered him to the school — his son, Michael, and I wandered down to Pelee Island's cemetery. It was a beautiful day, sunny and warm, and we walked along the rows on rows of fallen ancestors, war heroes, wine merchants, and farmers, marvelling at the wealth of history contained on such a small island. I was, by now, so well acquainted with Pelee's history that the names on the headstones were familiar to me. I recounted some of the more interesting tales to Michael.

At 4 p.m., Ted and Michael took the ferry back to Leamington, and I prepared for my final two weeks of solitude. I was determined to set aside some time alone to reflect on my journey. It was not to be.

Exactly 24 hours after he left, Ted was back. He had been suspended for a week from his job at *The Windsor Star* because he had used newspaper property for his personal use (in this case, the services of a newspaper technician to scan two of his freelance pictures, a practice that had previously been allowed). Just before he had been suspended, Ted had learned he had been nominated for two awards and had won an international honour. He was on a seesaw of elation and disgust. With disgust on the upswing, it hadn't taken much to convince Ted that there was no better place for him to lick his wounds than on Pelee. Just in case the ferry hadn't managed to ease his nerves, I ran out to the liquor store to get a couple of bottles of wine.

I shelved my plans for personal introspection to tend to Ted's bruised ego, but this interruption also forced me to confront a few issues that troubled me, and I used Ted as a sounding board.

Several days earlier, while we were out on a walk with our children, we spotted a rusted old car through the bushes along East West Road. When we took a closer look, we came across an alarming sight. All sorts of debris was scattered around a large area: a wrought-iron bed frame, machinery, cans filled with strange substances, hundreds of jars and bottles, pots, and pieces of scrap metal and ceramics. Michael found an old iron dating from the turn of the century. We later learned there were several areas on the island that had been popular dumping grounds.

Naturally, there were two regulated dumps on the island: one to dispose of household garbage, the other to dispose of large items such as refrigerators, stoves, mattresses, and machinery (this one was referred to by the islanders as "The Mall"). However, the old dump-sites unsettled me. Pelee was forging a reputation as an ecological wonder, but in two centuries of habitation no one had seriously addressed the issue of garbage or recycling. It seemed the township's council was content to let such things lie hidden from public view behind a bunch of bushes rather than clean up the mess. There were several houses where the owners had simply tossed their junk out their back door and left it there.

The Pelee Project

It wasn't the first time I felt politicized by what was happening on Pelee. There were other disturbing issues that triggered reactions in me that probably weren't befitting a person struggling to achieve a spiritual transformation.

I had heard gossip about islanders who refused to patronize the island's grocery store, preferring to make weekly trips by air or ferry to the mainland to do their shopping. So much for "making a commitment to the island." How, I wondered, could Pelee, of all places, expect to thrive when some of its inhabitants refused to patronize its main store? Yes, the prices were a bit higher — but not so high that it was worth spending $50 on a round-trip flight to the mainland. If some islanders were that small-minded, what were they doing on an island in the first place?

I had also heard stories about relatively recent episodes of feuding among islanders. In one incident, the anger had escalated to the point where someone had killed another person's dogs out of vengeance.

There were also murmurings about the reeve, who had lost his job at the liquor store. Some people thought he deserved it; others thought he didn't, not because he wasn't guilty but because "this is Pelee," as if the island had a papal dispensation to operate under a separate code of conduct. The good-ol'-boy attitude still prevailed on Pelee.

There was also trouble brewing over the island's septic and sewage system. For years, sewage had been dumped at a site on the east side of the island. New measures were being implemented, but many people were resisting the changes. Nobody seemed to be concerned about the threat of soil or water contamination.

When I brought all the incidents together, Pelee began to tarnish before my eyes. I wanted the island to be Eden, but it wasn't. I wanted people to work together to help the place succeed, and to aspire to a higher standard, but these goals weren't always being met. As I looked around, I began to see that Pelee Island was a microcosm of the same issues that plague and divide cities and towns everywhere. The revelation hit me smack in the face: Pelee Island wasn't much different than anywhere else; it was just smaller.

I felt silly and ashamed for having been so naïve. At the same time, my hands were tied: I couldn't really report on this side of Pelee because it wasn't relevant to the series I was writing for the *Post*. The series was about a spiritual retreat, it wasn't a political exposé. I was also reluctant to make waves with the islanders. They had been so generous to me, and I didn't want to lose their friendships.

I was now seeing a bit of Pelee's underbelly, and just as I did the shit hit the fan — literally. The septic system at Irma's house started malfunctioning. The quick thaw, I was told, had put pressure on the septic bed, causing it to flood. The stench was awful. Not only was our water discoloured from high iron levels, but now it was also twice as ugly, and I feared Zoë and I might get sick. Even though our drinking water was bottled, we brushed our teeth and washed our dishes with tap water. I cautioned Zoë and suggested we both be more vigilant. In addition, I told her, the flooding septic bed had aggravated the water pressure, preventing the toilet from flushing properly. It meant one thing: we had to use the outhouse. It wasn't as horrendous as we had thought it would be, just inconvenient. But the novelty wore off quickly — in about two days. Instead of counting the weeks to the end of our retreat, we began counting the days to when we could use a real toilet and indulge ourselves with a long, hot shower.

The island's problems worried me. Being an outsider had given me the distance to see where improvements could be made. But being an outsider also shut me out from participating in those changes.

Not knowing what to do, I turned my attention to our return to urban life. I began checking out summer camps for Zoë, I e-mailed the *Post* to remind my employer I was returning to work in a few weeks, I tidied up Irma's house and started packing our belongings, I reinstated my car insurance (there had been no need for it on Pelee). And I booked our final passage to the mainland. I arranged a few lunches with friends. I booked a tune-up for my car and a tune-up for myself at the spa I had frequented in Hamilton. I tried to psyche myself up for a hybrid Pelee-Hamilton routine.

I also had to face the harsh reality that, with the sale of our Hamilton house closing at the end of June, I had to find a home for us in Toronto. Although I had been born and raised in Toronto, the enchantment of living in a big city had diminished for me over the years, especially over the past few months. There was a lot to love about the city, but I didn't want to live in it. I couldn't picture myself there, and I couldn't see my children particularly liking it either. But my job was in Toronto, and, with the car accident still fresh in my mind, commuting was no longer an option.

I began scouting the newspapers in smaller towns in search of a job, but the editors at those papers were taken aback that I would trade a job at a national newspaper for one of less stature and at considerably less pay. Apparently, the concept was foreign to them. Life off the grid made for a really good story, but it didn't translate well into the "real world." I decided to hold off on my job search until Zoë and I were settled back home.

Zoë also had a to-do list during our remaining days on Pelee. Hers, thankfully, was easier to accomplish than mine. At the top of it was an excursion to Fish Point Provincial Nature Reserve. One of two conservation areas on Pelee (the other is at Lighthouse Point), Fish Point is the long, narrow sandbar that characterizes the island's southwest point. When you get to the tip of the spit, you are genuinely at the most southerly inhabited portion of Canada.

Our trek began along a log-bordered path through a dense forest. A sign at the entrance to Fish Point politely asked visitors to take nothing but pictures. Information markers highlighted particular plants or species we were likely to encounter.

It was a serene, almost ghostly place, a tangle of Carolinian vines and felled trees. As a summer tourist, I last saw this forest at the peak of its lush greenery. Other intrepid hikers and bikers were plentiful on the trail, and the forest was alive with activity and the chatter of birds.

The forest was stripped of all that on the dull spring day

The Pelee Project

Zoë and I visited it. We walked quietly — almost reverently — single file through a vista of varying shades of brown instead of a sea of green. At times, we stumbled across a branch of wild berries, and their colour screamed out in contrast to the beige surroundings. Occasionally, our silence was broken by the sound of a heron taking off from the marsh just beyond the forest's border, or by a flash of white as a cottontail darted in front of us.

As we wound our way through the scrub, our hands gently pushing aside an errant branch that threatened to blind us, I imagined this scenery wasn't much different than it was in 1838, when 400 Americans (variously described as patriots and pirates) used a frozen Lake Erie to sneak across from Sandusky and invade Pelee Island. The McCormicks fled the island, leaving behind their home and livestock, and alerted the British at Fort Malden (now the Ontario town of Amherstburg). The British returned to Pelee with a small army, and a battle for the island ensued. The battle began off the west shore of Fish Point in an area known as Mosquito Bay, and it spread into these very woods, where the ragtag invaders scattered as the infinitely more organized British troops set upon them. About a dozen soldiers on both sides were killed, but the invaders were defeated. The McCormicks faced a gruelling task in rebuilding their lives. Their home had been plundered and their livestock killed. Even the lamps from the island's new lighthouse — my beloved lighthouse! — were ripped out.

Zoë and I reached the end of the wooded path and found ourselves at Mosquito Bay — or what we presumed was

Mosquito Bay. It was so foggy we could only see a few metres in front of us. We definitely couldn't see the spit of Fish Point. It looked spooky out there, and I suggested to Zoë that we come back another day when the weather was better.

She would have none of it. "When are we going to come back?" she yelled angrily. "We're leaving in a week. If you want to stay here, fine, but I'm going to the end of Fish Point." With that, she stomped on ahead of me.

I had never seen anyone so stubborn except, of course, for that person who always stared back at me in the mirror. Being the dutiful mother I was, I followed meekly behind her. The fog was so thick I had no idea how far we had to go. Looking behind us, I had no way of gauging how far we had come. We were walking into oblivion.

About half an hour later, we made it. Breathless, bedraggled, and damp, we found the absolute end of the Fish Point spit. Zoë grabbed a piece of driftwood and stuck it into the sand like an explorer proudly claiming her rightful territory.

I snapped a picture of her, she smiled engagingly, but when our little photo op was finished a scowl returned to her face, and she stomped past me to begin the long trek back to the beach, into the forest, up the long, winding path, and back to our car. She was still miffed that I'd had the audacity to try to weasel out of a walk to the tip of the island just because it was foggy.

My mind returned to Fish Point's flash points. Fish Point was a precursor to another battle over Pelee Island's ecological preservation. Ever since government agents invaded the island armed with charts and tape measures in the early 1970s, the islanders had been divided over the issue. Environmental assessments put a stranglehold on development, which, depending on what side of the fence you sat on, was either a good thing or a bad thing.

In the city, environmental concerns give rise to equally thorny debates. But city dwellers witness environmental degradation every day. You just have to sit in rush-hour traffic to know where all those exhaust fumes are going. Add factory discharges, pesticides, and construction dust and you can understand why urban populations rail against such unhealthy air being breathed in in the name of progress. While cities solve the problem by spreading out and diffusing the impacts of environmental damage, islands can't.

Despite the heavy-handed approach, there were good aspects to the government's objectives. As I understood it, the plan would begin with a formal recognition of Pelee Island's uniqueness — species of flora and fauna needed to be documented and catalogued. Once they were identified, the opportunity existed to haul in all those Canadian and American tourists clamouring for eco-holidays: Pelee Island would be a perfect destination since it didn't require a passport. If the island's reputation could fuel the tourist trade, then it would bode well for the continuance of a sustainable community. The island would grow and flourish, and the population would cease to dwindle.

Finally, parts of Pelee would retain their historical or ecological designation in perpetuity, which I think adds to a community's pride and cachet. Pelee Islanders were all aware that their island held special ecological wonders, and to their credit they had managed to preserve those features largely on their own.

From what I heard, much of the government's intent was palatable to the majority of islanders, but when two words were added to the lexicon — blue racer — any hope of cooperation went out the window.

The blue racer is a species of snake unique to Pelee Island. The islanders were fine with having the snake identified, being instructed on the reptile's best natural habitat, and understanding how best to preserve the species — indeed, some islanders went to great lengths to make the snake feel at home on their property. But those good intentions backfired: government officials — referred to as the Snake People by the islanders — descended on Pelee and began to put restrictions on what owners could and could not do to their private property whenever a blue racer was spotted. Desperate to protect their property from being seized, many islanders not only stopped cooperating with the government, but some began killing the snakes whenever the slimy creatures showed up on their property.

A few days earlier, the lightning rod for this distrust, a young wildlife biologist named Ben, popped in to introduce himself to me. I had heard such alarming stories about the fracas over the blue racer that I wanted to meet the instigator. I was just praying he wouldn't be the kind of kook who carried a snake with him wherever he went. I don't like snakes.

Ben had fallen under Pelee's spell when he came to the island to work on his master's degree thesis in 1994. So taken was he with the island, he purchased about 40 hectares along Curry Dyke Road at the south end of Pelee. His dream was to turn the property into a wildlife sanctuary for snakes, and a sort of eco-school for elementary and high school students. I had walked past Ben's place every time I took my morning constitutional, but it was so far from the road that it looked like a hangout for the Branch Davidians, a kind of mini Waco.

Ben sat in my living room — snakeless, thank God — and tried to make sense of the brouhaha. The problem, he admitted, began with his thesis, which was about a passion of his: endangered species. His research was thorough and eventually found its way to the Ontario Ministry of Natural Resources and into the idle hands of some government wastrel who decided his mission in life would be to save and preserve the blue racer. Suddenly, property assessment notices began arriving in the mailboxes of the islanders announcing that property owners were eligible for tax relief if parts of their property were preserved as snake habitat. But tax relief wasn't important to Pelee Islanders; they wanted their property.

Naturally, the ministry, maintaining the long-standing government tradition of ignoring the concerns of law-abiding citizens, refused to come clean with its agenda. Instead of sitting down with the islanders and explaining its intentions, the government created an atmosphere of distrust and anger. The islanders' survival mechanism kicked in. As I soon found out, some of the islanders almost burst a blood vessel whenever talk turned to Pelee's ecological preservation.

Ben said he was astonished to see his thesis used in this way.

but since his name was on it, the islanders held him responsible for their predicament. To them, Ben and the government were one and the same. The tires on his car were slashed, he received death threats, and he was shunned by many of the islanders.

As I listened to Ben, I got to thinking: what the hell has all this got to do with a spiritual retreat? Why couldn't I just leave well enough alone? However there were lessons to learn from this — about the danger of riding roughshod over someone's sensibilities and property, and about the need to be flexible and forgiving.

I was no snake lover, but it seemed clear to me that someone in his youthful passion had begun a project with good intentions and had then been taken advantage of and ultimately misjudged. I couldn't understand why all the parties couldn't air their grievances and then work something out that could preserve both Pelee's natural beauty and the islanders' property rights. And if the islanders and Ben could work something out, then wouldn't they be stronger against the evil forces of the government?

Once again, I wanted Pelee to be perfect and peaceful. It annoyed me that both sides of this argument couldn't get their acts together and calmly deal with the issue before it erupted into the Hatfields versus the McCoys. Maybe Ben wasn't right; maybe the naysayers on the island weren't right either. But it was clear the stalemate was killing Pelee Island.

Chapter 17

A Good Friday Good-Bye

"That's all," said Humpty Dumpty. "Good-bye."
This was rather sudden, Alice thought: but after such a very strong hint
that she ought to be going, she felt that it would hardly be civil to stay.
— Through the Looking Glass *by Lewis Carroll*

Our last week.

Part of me couldn't believe our retreat was over; the other part of me couldn't wait until it was over. Saying good-bye had become as exhausting and overwhelming as greeting a long-lost friend — times 100. There were so many good-byes that after a while it was all I could do to muster a smile and make my sentiments sound genuine.

I thought back to my first week on Pelee — how alone I was, how unsure I was of what we were doing there, how we would fare emotionally, and how I got into such a tizzy over my search for milk. How ridiculous I was. Zoë could have survived a week, a month, three months without milk. And who knows? Maybe by now she would have been able to tell a merlot from a cabernet sauvignon.

Our transition had been easy and relatively painless, overall. And what did we have to show for it? I had a calmer demeanour, a better understanding of who I was, and the knowledge of what it took in this old world to make me happy. There were also subtle lessons learned along the way and, best of all, a long list of new friends and acquaintances. Even those islanders I didn't know particularly well hugged me good-bye. My heart and my mind were etched with memories of each one of them.

As I made the rounds, thanking them all for their hospitality, I collected a few souvenirs for my family and friends back home. Actually, I wanted to gather up the whole island and take it back with me. I looked around for a suitable memento for me and finally settled on a gold pendant in the shape of Pelee Island that I bought — after much deliberation because it cost nearly $100 — from the Trading Post. It represented the golden time I'd had on Pelee.

Early in the week, I phoned my sons to let them know when

we would be home, and my chat with Matt turned to the topic of summer jobs. At 15, he was too old for camp and too young to be hired by 7-11. I knew there were many opportunities for summer work on Pelee Island, but I had been reluctant to mention them to him since he had called the place "lame" on his first visit. Now, he said, he was "into it" and asked me if I could scout out something for him.

One such place was The Tin Goose, a bright mustard-coloured B&B at the end of East West Road. Kim, its effervescent manager, invited me to tour the place and give her the specs on Matt. Despite his young age, I assured her he was eager and reliable, and she asked me to bring him in for an interview in a few weeks.

I phoned Matt with the news. If he had been unhappy about my leaving him for three months to find myself, he was ecstatic that the ordeal had at least produced the promise of a summer job for him.

Meanwhile, Zoë and I continued to battle the septic system at our island home. The water had become so bad that we wondered whether it was wise to even shower in it. It had been days, in fact, since we had properly bathed, and we were still using the outhouse. The stench from the sewage seeping into the basement from the septic bed was getting stronger. By midweek, we'd had enough. We were booked to leave Pelee on Sunday — Easter Sunday — but I got on the phone and moved our departure up to Good Friday instead.

There was irony to this, I found. As I related our woes to Mary Lou, she laughed. "Do you not see how funny that is?"

she said. "The island's telling you that life is shitty here too!"

In fact, it almost seemed like the island was forcing me out, as if I had learned my lessons and overstayed my welcome. Maybe the fact that I had started to see the underbelly of Pelee Island had rubbed Mr. Island the wrong way.

With our departure mere days away, Mary Lou, whose work involves rituals, suggested Zoë and I appease the island and bid it a formal farewell in a ceremony she would devise. All we had to do, she said, was pick our favourite part of Pelee and bring a gift for the island.

The next morning at 7:15, Zoë and I drove to a clearing on South Shore Road. During my own daily ritual, I had walked past this spot many times. As the weather had warmed up, I had veered from the road occasionally and walked along the flat and smooth rock surface that formed the beach along this segment of Pelee. I thought this would be a good place to say good-bye.

Mary Lou was already there. She had told us to dress up — "It's a farewell party, after all," she had enthused. I dressed as best I could given my extremely casual black wardrobe. Zoë was dressed for school. But Mary Lou looked like the elegant witch she was: long, flowing, multicoloured skirt; layers of colourful sweaters; black boots; and all of it topped with a wizardly looking cape of green boiled wool. She was even decked out in mesmerizing earrings and heavy necklaces. And she was holding maracas.

"This is for you," she said, giving one to Zoë. "This is a celebration of your time on Pelee, and we're going to make some noise about it!"

She asked me to choose a noisemaker, so I picked another rattle. I was beginning to feel a bit goofy, as was Zoë. But we were in Mary Lou's hands now.

"Oh, Goodness and Energy of the Universe," she intoned to the sky, her arms raised as a gorgeous fiery ball peeked over the horizon, "I summon you in the name of Jane and Zoë." After her dramatic incantation, she turned to us with instructions. "I want each of you to face a direction and offer a prayer that addresses the fears and hopes that direction represents. You can say anything you want. Then repeat this for each of the four compass points: north, south, east, and west."

Zoë looked at me.

"You go first," I said.

"No, you!" she urged between clenched jaws.

We were facing south, so I offered my prayer to the south — to its promise of warmth and tranquillity, qualities I always felt whenever I ventured south to lands where palm trees swayed langorously, where the warm, azure water cleansed me of my worries and invited me to play, and where the soft breezes felt like a gentle massage on my neck and shoulders.

Then I faced west. I was stumped here at first, but I remembered how the ferry had delivered me to the West Dock on my first visit, so I gave thanks to the ferry and to the lake for having spirited me to Pelee Island those many months ago.

I turned to face the north and stood staring into Pelee Island itself. There was a lot to be thankful for here. "Thank you for welcoming Zoë and me to this land, for keeping us safe, and for allowing us to enjoy the luxury of time and of silence. And now we leave knowing so many beautiful people and being thankful for the lessons they taught us."

I looked beyond Pelee's north shore and imagined Canada, my home and my native land. A land that I love, that I appreciate, and that I thank God for each day (despite the uninspiring and soulless leadership of its government — though I didn't add that).

Finally, I faced east, and I felt my heart tremble. In the east lay Toronto, where so many good and decent people become swallowed up in the shadow of greed and big deals and I'm-too-busy-to-talk-to-you brush-offs. Here I asked for strength to help me stay strong against the overwhelming tower of power, to remember the lessons I had learned, and to remain true to my heart and to my heart's desires.

I turned to Zoë, and she began by facing east. "East is where my home is in Hamilton, and I can't wait to go back and see my friends and my family. When I face south, I will always think about the nature on Pelee Island, especially at Fish Point. I had so much fun. I felt free."

She faced north: "I thank the north because my Pelee Island school is at the north end. I remember my first day of school and how nervous I was. But people were really nice to me, and I made some friends. So I'm grateful to the north for letting me go to school here."

Finally, facing west, she said, "When I think of the west, I think of the day Mom brought me to Pelee Island for the first time. I was excited to see the island and to visit a new place."

Mary Lou then asked us to present our gifts to the island. I had written a note of gratitude on a small piece of (biodegradable) paper. I tore it up, threw it into the air, and let it flutter like confetti over the water and into the many crevices that lined the shore. Zoë had collected some rocks from the island during our stay, and now she returned them to it, throwing a few into the lake, placing others along the rivulets that spread like fingers into the rocky beach. The sun was fully up, and its early rays twinkled like stars on the gentle waves that lapped around our feet.

Following Mary Lou's lead, we took our various noise-makers and gave wild whoops and chants as we shook our rattles and leaped and danced around the beach with abandon. Out of the corner of my eye, I saw a truck drive slowly past this Druid-like spectacle and wondered whether it would be fodder at the next Legion soirée. I didn't care. Our spirited trio had a lot to celebrate, including the gift of a new friendship.

Mary Lou offered a final prayer of thanks to God for bringing Zoë and me to Pelee Island, for the pleasure of our company, and for the promise of safe passage back to Hamilton. She then presented us with gifts of amber, her favourite scent, and a necklace for each of us — necklaces that had sentimental value to her and contained, she assured us, magical qualities.

We hugged her good-bye. I knew I would miss the leisurely afternoons we had shared each week. Her laugh had raised my spirits, and her wisdom had invigorated me, giving me the courage to move forward on those days when I had doubted myself.

Zoë and I drove back to the house. It was time for her to get ready for school.

"Gee," I said to her. "How many kids get to start their day with a farewell ritual? Are you going to tell your friends about it?"

"Mom!" she admonished me. "But," she added, "it was kind of fun, wasn't it? I felt silly at first, but it was neat to have our own private ceremony."

Zoë was preparing her own good-byes to her school. She was excited about returning to her many friends in Hamilton the following week, but I could tell she felt torn about where her heart lay. She had developed a routine here, and the chance to be herself, to run free and to know her mother was waiting at home for her, was intoxicating for her. She had completed an academic term on Pelee Island, and she had a report card — an exceedingly good one — as a memento. I was so proud of her as I watched her get on the bus for the last time. Such a resilient, determined, and delightful child.

I thanked Grant for being such a faithful bus driver, and then I turned around and took my final walk around the block. As I passed personal totems along the way, my eyes filled with tears. It was hard to accept that this wouldn't be part of my routine anymore. When I returned home, I finished cleaning the house and collected our laundry.

Gail invited me over for tea. She was frantically getting Twin Oaks ready for her summer guests. The bookings had been coming in at a steady rate. We spoke about journalism. Gail was on a leave of absence from her job at *The Windsor Star*, and was evasive about whether she would return to it. She didn't want to go back, and I urged her not to. The business was changing and hardly resembled the profession on which we had based our careers and aspirations. If she went back to it, I told her, I would personally drag her back to Pelee. I envied her being able to be on the island all the time, and I wondered whether Ted and I could find happiness and success running an island B&B. Then I thought about which one of us was more likely to get stuck with the cooking and cleaning.

Gail's stepchildren, Kaeleigh and Kieran, were arriving that afternoon for Easter weekend. Gail asked if the children could get together one last time with Zoë.

I returned home to my chores and to prepare dinner. I had invited Dick and Franny and Dan over for our last supper together.

Dinner was at 5:30, the normal Pelee time for dinner, and while I'd had visions of a riotously drunk evening it was anything but. Everyone was in a pensive mood. We ate and shared wonderful memories of the past three months.

"Darlin'," said Dan, "we know why you had to come here, and we want you to know that if life ever gets too much for you again you always have a home on Pelee Island. Anytime you want to escape, all you have to do is let us know what ferry you'll be on. We'll be there to pick you up and take you in."

I didn't think hostesses were supposed to cry, so I suppressed my tears. I thanked them deeply for having looked after us. Like others on the island, they had been unfailingly generous. I promised to keep in touch and implored them to do the same.

Then, before I knew it, they were gone. It was only 7:30

p.m., just about bedtime on Pelee. I was thankful I hadn't had to direct anyone to the outhouse.

Zoë was looking at me expectantly. She was itching to see Kaeleigh and Kieran. "Mom, I know we have to leave early tomorrow, but can they stay overnight? It's the last time I'll see them. I promise we'll get up early."

They were true to their word. All three were up and dressed the next morning by seven o'clock.

I packed up the remaining groceries, and when Jim arrived to collect his children I gave him what was left in our pantry. I took a final snapshot of the three children leaning against the tree near the back door. The morning sun was golden and warm.

We said good-bye. What symmetry, I thought: Jim was the first islander I met when Zoë and I stepped off the plane that January afternoon, and he was the last islander I was saying good-bye to. I was reminded of our first meeting and how I had based my impression of him on third-hand information, from several colleagues. In fact, Jim had proved to be one of the kindest, gentlest, and most helpful people I had met. During the entire time I was on Pelee Island, he never said an unkind word about the *Post* or its management, at least not to my face, and he'd had ample opportunity to do so, even when Ted and I had invited him and Gail over for dinner and plied them with wine. I felt bad that I had allowed others to influence my initial attitude toward Jim and that I had prejudged him.

Zoë and I got into our car, and I started the engine. Then I turned the car off and ran back into the house: I wanted to water the plants one last time.

On our way to the ferry, we made a deposit at the dump: we were taking our newspapers back to the mainland to recycle them. We drove north along Pelee's west coast, sucking up the scenery and imprinting it on our memories. We uttered silent good-byes to our familiar haunts.

For some reason, the ferry was leaving from Scudder Dock at the north end. We drove up to the *Pelee Islander* and let one of the crew squeeze our car onto the deck. Zoë and I walked up to the top deck to admire the view and watch the beauty of the day unfurl.

"Hey, you!"

We looked down and saw a waving Franny on the pier. We scrambled back down the stairs. She wanted to bid us a final good-bye. We hugged and promised to write, to call, to visit. I asked her to say good-bye to Georgina for me at the Easter Sunday service.

I had expected a quiet, solemn ride back to the mainland, but we found Sondi behind the counter of the lounge's canteen furiously trying to finish a sweater she was knitting as a gift to her mother. Michelle and Paul and their little boys were also on board — they were off to visit her parents for Easter — and Amanda was there too. The nonstop chatter didn't give me a chance to pause and let the occasion sink in. Before we knew it, we were docked at Leamington.

We said more good-byes and drove our car off the boat and into Leamington's still-quiet streets. Neither Zoë nor I said much to each other. We were lost in our own thoughts.

I had an urge to drive directly to Hamilton, but I wanted to say good-bye to Ted, who was leaving for Tucson the next morning with his brother. Yet another farewell.

At about 10 p.m., Zoë and I rolled quietly into the driveway of our home in Hamilton.

"Let's leave the bags and stuff until the morning," I said.

We unlocked the front door and, as if in a trance, walked through the darkened house, upstairs, and into our beds.

The next morning, I heard cars honking and buses braking at their various stops. I opened my eyes and was momentarily disoriented without the familiar view of the fields stretching beyond East West Road. Instead, my eyes rested on my open clothes closet and a lonely pair of Manolo Blahniks. They looked as incongruous to my life as my Day-Timer had on my first morning on Pelee Island. I felt like Dorothy awaking from her odyssey to Oz. Had it all been a dream?

"Zoë!" I cried out.

She, too, had woken up disoriented.

If nothing else, we were grateful that we had an indoor bathroom to use.

As Zoë showered, I walked around my home, which now looked so strange to me. I couldn't believe how much I owned. Yet I had missed none of it while I was away.

I spent the day calling my boys and my mother to tell them we had arrived home safely. We would see them the next day, on Easter Sunday.

I unpacked, did laundry, and hooked up the computer. I checked my phone messages, but I couldn't speak to anyone. I was in a state of shock. I was unable to articulate where I had been, much less the impact of what I had experienced. I felt my throat constrict at the thought of doing so. I began to cry uncontrollably, as if I was grieving the loss of — of what? I couldn't put my finger on it. I hadn't lost anything, I had gained so much. Every time I looked at the clock, I wondered what my friends on Pelee Island were doing at that moment. I robotically performed the necessary chores around the house. I had no house plants to water.

On Easter Sunday, Zoë went with her dad to visit his family, eager to share her experiences with them and to report that she had lost a total of eight teeth during her Pelee stay.

Adam and Matt arrived at my house shortly after.

"Hey," said Matt.

"Hey," I replied.

We hugged, and I gave them the souvenirs we had brought back for them. The next thing I knew, Adam and Matt were settled on the couch in our family room watching TV. My absence seemed to have been little more than a blip in their lives. How much some things change, I thought, and how much other things remain the same.

Chapter 18

POST PELEE

Life is either a daring adventure, or nothing.
— Helen Keller

In my hands, I held a manila envelope that sagged under the weight of its contents. Inside was the detritus of my wallet, contents I had removed before our trip to Pelee Island: business cards, credit cards, a swipe card that allowed me into the company parking lot, another swipe card that allowed me into the office building, several frequent-saver cards, a library card, insurance cards. How many cards does one person need?

I arranged the cards in my urban wallet, then pulled them all out. I threw half of them away. I didn't need frequent-saver cards because I was no longer a frequent buyer. Possibly, our frivolous spending habits peak when our wallets and purses are weighed down with cards and riffraff. When you feel weighed down, you tend to shop more to give yourself a "lift." But when your wallet is lighter, and you have less physical encumbrances, the thought of weighing down your arms with packages and bags seems to be at odds with your hard-won freedom.

My wallet on Pelee was light; in fact, I only needed to carry cash. There was no police officer on the island during the winter and thus no need to carry my driver's licence. I paid for almost all my purchases by cash, so I never needed my bank card. Without such things, I managed to simplify even my wallet. (One of the true freedoms of Pelee was that I never had to carry a purse — ever.)

It took a while for Zoë and I to fully recover from our return to urban life. We never used a dishwasher on Pelee Island; we washed all our dishes by hand. It was a luxury to use our dishwasher again. But while the dishwasher replaced a chore, it also replaced the rambling conversation Zoë and I had in front of our Pelee sink — the sort of chats that come easily when your hands are swirling around in warm, foamy water.

Zoë slipped back into her routine and for a while we

regularly compared our urban life to our Pelee life. I was grateful that she could at least see the difference, and I hoped the experience taught her the value of resilience and of following your heart even when others are betting on your failure. She didn't learn how to make soup or muffins from scratch, but she showed me that I had taught her well about the need for daily rituals and traditions. When I was flailing about early in our retreat, she anchored me with simple rituals, such as lighting candles at dinner — even on school nights. She seamlessly carried on this task when we returned home, and I wondered whether she did this to keep a little of our Pelee ways in her heart. Wonder of wonders, she began to wear her hair off her face, without a single word from me.

I resumed my urban routine, but I didn't resume my medication or my shopping or my list-making or my gotta-do-it-all approach to life. It was hard to accept fences, sight lines impeding sunrises and sunsets, crowded residential streets, and streetlights that made it hard for me to sleep at night. I felt like a prisoner. Everything moved at warp speed, but I stood strong against the current and resisted the fast lane. I consciously allowed myself to stop, assess the chaos, and slow down. I was constantly out of step with those around me, but I didn't let it worry me. When cars roared up to my bumper, I either switched lanes or stubbornly stayed where I was. Let him or her move, I thought. I refused to permit anyone to dictate my speed.

I worked hard to filter out the visual and aural distractions of daily life, fearing that by even acknowledging them I would be sucked back into the same vortex I had struggled to escape months before. At times, the signs and the traffic lights and the long seductive aisles of food in grocery stores would rattle me so much that I began to cry. I was terribly confused about which world I should inhabit, yet I didn't feel as though I belonged wholly to either one.

I kept reading my Bible. I didn't need to make it a priority in my day-to-day life; I just accepted it as a vital part of my existence. I also continued to listen to Eminem.

I met up with my friend Kathie in Toronto for dinner and a show. As I walked along Bloor Street, I felt an overwhelming urge to scream out against the excess around me. I still considered myself a capitalist, but did it all have to look so crass? In the restaurant, Kathie looked so sophisticated sitting across from me, and I wondered whether I looked like a bumpkin to her. I had pared down my makeup, and my hairstyle lacked even a smidgen of style. I felt awkwardly slow as everyone hustled around me, and I had trouble keeping up with Kathie as we walked to the theatre.

I gradually reconnected with my friends, who were eager to share their thoughts about my adventure. However, I was more interested to know what they had been up to. I had become better at listening than at talking.

Gradually, the person who had walked so freely along South Shore Road began drifting, and I had to struggle to hold on to her. I found an old copy of the *New Yorker*. On its cover was an illustration of a little girl on a beach holding a conch shell to her ear while adults hovered in the background holding cellphones to their ears. I framed it as a reminder never to lose a sense of child-like wonder.

I established a daily walk in my neighbourhood. I doubt it was seven kilometres long, but it was a walk nonetheless. I made up a route that took me through residential areas, up to a park, through a wooded area, back through a residential area, and then home. It was only in the woods that I felt free to be me; I could almost feel my feet skip knowing I was off the beaten path. I was never a nature girl, but now I looked up at the trees soaring above me, and I understood the comparison of forests to cathedrals. I felt more at home in the woods than I did on the city streets. When my route returned me to the pavement, I drew back into myself like a turtle withdrawing into its shell.

I looked at the cars to see whether I could recognize anyone, but most of them had tinted windows, so I couldn't see the drivers. No one honked hello, so I didn't wave. The same sense of anonymity ruled the sidewalks. But at least there were surprises. Just when I gave up saying "Hello" to people who didn't respond, a few brave strangers initiated a "Good morning," and it brightened me up. Maybe cities weren't lost causes after all.

A week later, I returned to work. My colleagues congratulated me on the series, though one person admitted he didn't like "the God bits." Some asked whether I had used the sabbatical as a way to hide a face-lift. I assured them there had been no surgery, and I felt insulted they had thought I even needed a face-lift. Others commented on my appearance. "Your hair's grown." "Is that a new outfit?" "Did you lose weight?" Why is it that women can't greet one another without commenting on the other's weight? Not one person said, "Wow, your soul looks so refreshed and peaceful." But several did mention that my face looked rested and that I smiled more and looked happy. Maybe the face really is the mirror of the soul.

Everyone noticed I had slowed down, and I think it became a bit of an office joke. I used to power-walk through the office; I now moved as if I was recovering from a bypass operation.

If I was feeling displaced in the outside world, I was feeling just as displaced in my work environment. A *Post* executive sat me down and politely asked what I wanted to do now that I was back at work. I told him I would like to write, and asked if I might have hours that were conducive to the needs of my children. I was promptly placed on the night editing desk, where the shift began at 4 p.m. and ended at midnight.

Despite the demotion at work, I didn't lose my cool. In my previous life, I would have kicked up a fuss. I accepted the change and the fact that I worked for an employer who didn't treat sabbaticals as opportunities for employees to expand their creativity or to observe the world in action. Sadly, to most employers, sabbaticals are considered a sign of weakness and a lack of commitment to the corporate good. How wrong they are. But the adjective "brave" that my colleagues had affixed to me before I left for Pelee Island was, indeed, code for "career suicide."

As I write this, I am sitting at a table in my kitchen watching the snow fall. It is almost the end of January, and it has been an unseasonably mild and snowless winter. But now the snow is accumulating on the cold, bare branches. The sky is white, the snow is white. There are birds flitting from branch to branch. I can pick out a sparrow, a cardinal, a few grackles. Winter has descended on us again.

A year ago, I looked out at an entirely different scene in an entirely different world. It was a tumultuous year, but never were there better tests to reinforce the lessons I had learned on Pelee Island or to prove whether I had paid attention in my island classroom. Not that there weren't missteps.

After my return to urban life, I sucked up my courage and began to look for a home in Toronto. In a city of three million people, one wouldn't think that would be hard to do, but it was. With so many neighbourhoods to choose from, I settled on one in the east end of the city, an area known as The Beaches. As its name implies, it is situated along the north shore of Lake Ontario, an older neighbourhood that, more than a century ago, was considered cottage country for Torontonians. After gagging on the price that a small, semi-detached home commands in the area, I justified it by the fact that I would at least have a home near the lake and no longer have an arduous commute to work. But I didn't want to move to Toronto. It felt wrong. My instincts told me it was wrong.

When the deal closed on my Hamilton house and I still hadn't found a place to live, I shipped our belongings into storage and moved in with my mother. Those who have moved back in with their parent(s) — even temporarily — know that the experience is fraught with mixed emotions. On the one hand, my mother cared for me so well I wondered whether I even wanted to get a place of my own. On the other hand, it was like surrendering my adulthood. I felt like a failure to myself and to my children. I had worked so hard all my life only to end up, euphemistically, "living at home."

As the summer wore on, I got a little too accustomed to wearing house dresses and engaging in afternoon cribbage games with Mom. Since I didn't start work until 4 p.m., she asked me if I would like to learn how to play bridge and join her friends for lunchtime tournaments. I checked to see whether I owned a strand of pearls.

Throughout the summer, Pelee Island was never far from my sights, and Ted and I returned as summer tourists and rented a cottage for two weeks. Matt got a summer job there and thrived. By the time I returned to Pelee at the end of August to collect him, he didn't want to leave the island. It was strange to see him in my old world. He mourned his departure for months after and announced he was going to return the following summer. He, too, had felt the tug.

Eventually, I found a home in Toronto with the help of Wes, a patient and hilariously over-the-top real estate agent. More than once he asked me, "Are you *sure* you really want to move here?" I wasn't sure, but it seemed to be the most expedient thing to do. I bought the house, but it felt wrong. A month later, we moved in, but it still felt wrong. I masked all doubts by launching into redecorating schemes and making frequent forays to join the bustle on Queen Street, but it still felt wrong.

Two weeks later, still not fully out of boxes, I lost my job. The *Post* was "downsizing" and "converging" and "ramping up" all at the same time. Now I understood why it had all felt wrong. Every bone and organ in my body had warned me against the move, but I had forged ahead. I faced the consequences of not having listened to my instincts.

I scrambled to find another job, but the market was contracting, and the havoc and fear inflicted on the world by a band of terrorists whom no one had heard of before left the planet reeling. Amid such profound global horror, I retreated and pulled myself together. This was way bigger than my loss, I assured myself. As the calamity and the finger-pointing raged, I stopped my job hunt and waited and listened.

Eventually, work — not full-time but work nonetheless — trickled in. Gradually, I viewed my layoff as a gift from God. He had allowed me to escape the rat race and to reset my compass. I faced enforced simplicity of an entirely different nature, but it didn't frighten me; it intrigued me. When things went wrong or didn't come through the way I had expected, I sat down and quietly listened to the lesson. Instead of feeling wronged or rejected, I felt guided by my inner voice. Sometimes things happen for a reason, and sometimes they don't. I am now listening to that voice, not to the voices of an urgent, fear-mongering society. I no longer go along with how the world says I should live.

One day, while I was cleaning up my backyard, I found a plant that had been abandoned by the previous owners of my home, and I took it inside. I water it weekly, and it is thriving and flowering. I have limited my houseplants to one so as not to overload my precious expertise.

My children are back to fighting with each other. No amount of yelling from me can convince them to stop, so I've stopped yelling and allow them to take responsibility for their own bruises. I don't take any medication, not even vitamins, and I feel as healthy as a middle-aged mom with no fixed employment can. I refuse to join the coffee culture that has spread to epidemic proportions in the city. I can't seem to find a Norm or a Mary Lou with whom to share a cuppa. I don't patronize any place that promises fast anything. I rarely venture to places where the rushing masses congregate except when I want cheap amusement. I pass homeless people, toss my loonies into their cups, and stop and chat with them. They are reminders of the need to be humble and charitable in a capricious world where a person's fortunes can alter in a second.

Although the "Toronto experiment" didn't work out, it, too, was a valuable lesson, one I needed to be retaught. It was a reminder to let my instincts, and not the wishes of others, guide me. I heard this reiterated by a minister when I attended the funeral of a friend's mother: when God wants to teach you a truth, he implants it not in your intellect but in your instinct.

At Christmas, I flew to Pelee Island with Ted. The airplane was the same, but the airport had changed (the plane now flew out of Windsor rather than Leamington), and there were strict security measures — even for a 12-minute flight.

Bev lent us her East Shore Road home for our three-day visit. It was a working holiday for both of us, but Ted uncharacteristically dragged me away from my laptop on Christmas Eve to attend the carol service at the old Methodist-turned-United-turned-Anglican church. It was packed — a rare but heartwarming sight. Georgina was absent so George led the service, students from PIPS read the lessons, and Deb, the school bus driver, was at the piano playing the familiar hymns as our voices sang heartily on that dark, clear, and cold night.

Christmas Day was the strangest I had ever experienced. It was the first one I spent without my family, without a Christmas tree, without a turkey roasting in the oven, without boughs framing a fireplace mantel or white mini lights twinkling everywhere, without giddy children running through the house or prying open tightly wrapped gifts. A wave of melancholy washed over me as I looked at a cold, blue-grey Lake Erie and a barren landscape. But it was also the first Christmas I spent completely conscious that this was a day to honour the birth of a child whose life and death had revolutionized our spiritual selves. I felt a reverence for the day that I had never felt.

I thought back to where I was a year earlier, preparing and packing for an odyssey that would transform me, though at the time I knew not how, or even if, it would happen. And now I sat in a quiet house on Christmas Day overloaded with invisible gifts I appreciated so much: the gift of recovered senses; the gift of inhaling life; the gift of silence so I could hear the birds sing and my heart speak; the gift of being touched and taught by strangers; and the gift of resurrected instincts that had brought me to a seemingly unremarkable island so that it could work its remarkable magic on me.

THERE OUGHT TO BE A LAW

Hunters are usually given specific seasons in which to hunt.
Those hunting for simple ideas may benefit from the focus
of a specific "thinking" season.
— Edward de Bono

I received hundreds of e-mails from people asking how they could take a simple spiritual retreat like the one I took. Before I give you some guidelines, it's important to clarify what such a retreat is and what simplicity really means.

Simplicity does not come in a neat little box. It means more than cutting back on material possessions, doing without fancy linens and housewares, or slowing down. Simplicity doesn't come from a store or a magazine. It comes from within.

Yes, paring down material possessions is part of the game — but only if you feel unnecessarily burdened by them. Getting rid of your dishes so that you can buy new, cream-coloured dishes isn't simplicity — it's consumerism. If you want to buy cream-coloured dishes, then by all means do so. Just don't try to rationalize your purchase as a move toward simplicity.

Go ahead and buy used clothing, hold on to items until they wear out, use cash instead of credit cards, learn to say no, and cut out the superfluous busyness in your life. These measures are all well and good, but they don't necessarily add up to simplicity. Simplicity is less about denying yourself things (though it's not about rampant materialism, either) and more about the priorities you set and how you deal with the world. Ultimately, the right priorities and approaches will result in enduring spiritual regeneration, as well as a less-cluttered life — and I mean "cluttered" in both a material and emotional sense.

Make sure you are taking your sabbatical/retreat for the right reasons. It's not an escape; it's a way to renew yourself and reconnect with a more balanced life. A retreat won't magically remove an abusive husband or a messy divorce or an annoying in-law. The best a retreat can do is give you distance from the problem *temporarily* so you can come to a solution without the distractions of daily life.

OK, enough of the sermon. Here are a few guidelines for planning your retreat.

1. If you decide that a retreat is really what you need, plan on spending a minimum of three months, but preferably four or five months. You'll need that much time to empty yourself of your previous patterns of behaviour, adjust to the emptiness, and begin the slow and steady rebuilding of your inner self. Jesus may have been able to do it in 40 days and 40 nights, but lesser mortals need more time. We would all like to go from den mother to Zen mother overnight or over a weekend, but it's not going to happen. It takes about four weeks to rid your body and mind of your urban routine and anxieties. You will feel angry, bitter, cantankerous, depressed . . . you will pretty much go through the alphabet of emotions. This is both normal and cathartic.

2. Find a quiet place where you can contemplate your life. Choose somewhere that isn't distracting, some-where that may even be difficult for others to reach. Islands are good choices because they keep you contained; you're less likely to stray into a neighbouring town or city. People wondered why I didn't conduct my retreat during the summer. The reason was that I'm as hopeless as the next person: give me a

hot, sunny beach, and I'm there with a blanket, a book, and a beer, spiritual rejuvenation be damned. In contrast, a stark terrain and generally miserable, cold weather are optimal for a spiritual retreat. Oddly enough, growth and transformation take place under such conditions.

3. Your children won't understand why you have to go. Your spouse may not understand either, or even want you to go. Your friends will think you're having a midlife crisis. If a retreat is something you believe will make a real difference in your life, if it's what your heart truly desires, then do it. If your family members say they can't or won't stand behind you while you take a breather for a few months, go anyway. Let them learn to live without you for a while. (I highly recommend Ann Tyler's *Ladder of Years*, the story of a woman who basically takes off her apron, walks out on her family, and goes to live in another town under a new identity.) My sons lived without me, and they learned to be more resilient in my absence (and perhaps a bit more appreciative of my presence). My mother learned to live without me too. When I returned after three months, she had made some startling realizations about herself: "I knew I couldn't depend on you when you were away," she told me. "I was upset at first, but I discovered that I

am strong enough on my own. It's not that I don't need you, it's just that I found the will to get on with living." When I did return, I was a much more understanding and patient person. The paradox of such retreats is that it's only by leaving those you love that you can truly give yourself to them.

4. By all means, take one of your school-age children with you. Get your child away from video games (an insidious and soul-destroying diversion) and let him or her breathe fresh air, crawl through muddy culverts, and learn to appreciate nature. Zoë gained so much from our retreat. Conversely, she taught me things about myself that I had been too busy to notice. If you do take a child with you, make sure your destination has a school, and call ahead to introduce yourself and your child. You'll need to take a copy of your child's most recent report card. While I'm not opposed to home schooling, a spiritual retreat really isn't the occasion to do this. You can be certain this retreat will strengthen the bond between you and your child.

5. Take some books you've been longing to read, some videos for cuddle times on cold winter nights, a few board games, a few CDs, and a boombox on which to play them. Clothing should be totally functional and unrestrictive:

sweaters, sweatshirts, T-shirts, leggings, lots of
heavy socks, walking boots, a parka, heavy gloves,
a balaclava, and a scarf. If you are going to a
remote location and there isn't a phone, take a
cellphone. But only use it for calling out. Don't
give people your phone number, or they will
abuse your time.

6. A retreat needn't be expensive. In fact, if it is
expensive, it's not a retreat — it's a holiday.
There are organizations popping up that are in
the sabbatical business: they charge about
$6,000 (US) for a three-month retreat. So be
warned and beware of such schemes. Planning
it yourself gives you control over your time, and
allows you to give thought to what you're
doing. Expect to spend about $1,000 a month
to cover rent, bills (heat, hydro, phone), food,
and sundries. I was also carrying the mortgage
and bills on my urban home, so the financial
burden was heavier. I was lucky and thankful to
have a mother who generously bailed me out. I
paid her back. In the end, I figured, my retreat
cost nearly $5,000, which included my urban
expenses and responsibilities. That amount,
coincidentally, was exactly the amount of my
tax return that year. Never was my money better
spent. The financial press will urge you to use
such windfalls to top up your RRSP. Ignore them

— at least for one year. You need to live in the present, not in the future. If you really want to do something, you'll find a way to pay for it.

7. Don't expect to be turned into an angel by the end of your retreat. I'm a hopelessly flawed woman who still swears (though not nearly as much as I once did), doesn't floss, and forgets to say her prayers. I haven't developed an ethereal aura, nor do I have the Big Answers to the Big Questions. I'm a long way from being the kind of Christian I strive to be. But I try. Understand, too, that a belief in God is essential to finding your soul. If you've strayed off your spiritual path, that's fine; if you've lost God along the way, that's fine too. Just leave the door open, and He will find you.

8. Arrange for the time off work, and be prepared for resistance. You may have to enlist your family doctor as a partner in crime: medical leaves are easier for companies to swallow than lifestyle sabbaticals. Although sabbaticals have been common practice in the academic world since the late 19th century, they fall in and out of fashion in the corporate world.

   The benefits of sabbaticals for both employee and employer are evident and well-documented — albeit largely anecdotally — but many organizations (private and public) not only struggle with the concept, they are largely resistant to the idea, judging by their lack of action. In 1994, the federal government struck an advisory committee that recommended the work week be cut by 10%, and job-sharing and gradual-retirement programs be considered. As I said, that was in 1994. We are no closer to any of those recommendations.

In the corporate world, sabbaticals are used as a retention tool to entice new recruits or to keep existing ones. There has been no effort to reduce working hours or redistribute the work. There has been no movement on a proposal suggested by Frank Reid at the University of Toronto, who called for legislation that would bestow upon the individual the right to choose shorter hours.

Instead, the opposite is true: individuals are working longer hours, and they are tethered to Palm Pilots, computers, e-mail, cellphones, voice messaging, and fax machines. Resist the slavish trend to wire yourself to your employer. To do so contributes to the work-and-spend treadmill of stressed-out, time- impoverished people. When you work more, you spend more, and when you buy more you become tied down by debt and possessions. This is the antithesis of the New Simplicity movement. No wonder the corporate culture delicately discourages the notion of sabbaticals.

The reality is, you will probably be the one to make the first move when broaching the idea of a sabbatical with your employer. You may even be the only person who has asked for one. Don't be afraid. Every movement needs trailblazers. Recognize that your company, like all companies, is in the business of making money, not giving employees time off. If you are too frightened to take a sabbatical because you fear a workplace reprisal, then maybe it's time to evaluate why you are working for that employer in the first place.

9. There were a number of books I found particularly useful during my retreat. They are not how-to guides per se, but they do impart a type of wisdom that shows you there is more than one way of living and looking at life.

• *Spiritual Renewal Bible* (Tyndale House Publishers, 1998): This dynamic version strengthened my faith, and its many insights, notes, and lessons on how a particular passage of scripture relates to modern life made me realize that spiritual or emotional depletion is something with which many people struggle. Plus, it's such a readable text that you'll soon be reaching for it constantly just so you can find out what happens next to

Esther, Mordecai, and King Xerxes. Who knew the Bible could be such a great read?

- *The Monk Who Sold His Ferrari*, by Robin Sharma (Harper Perennial, 1997): A spiritual fable that is a bit hokey at times, but it nonetheless imparts some eye-opening lessons.
- *Anatomy of the Spirit*, by Caroline Myss (Three Rivers Press, 1996): This was the book that first put me on my spiritual path. A hairdresser recommended it to me, and it totally changed the way I looked at emotional and physical ailments. It is a remarkable book. Along with the Bible mentioned above, it is a vital resource, to which I frequently refer.
- *Simplicity*, by Edward de Bono (Viking, 1998): A quirky but fascinating book that looks at the concept of simplicity from a philosophical point of view.
- *The Career Guide for Creative and Unconventional People*, by Carol Eikleberry (Ten Speed Press, 1999): For anyone who ever felt like a square peg in a round world. Our everyday stresses can sometimes be the result of bad fits with our jobs. People who want to veer off the beaten track usually don't work well on assembly lines or follow orders well (for the simple reason that they have better ideas than the people for whom they work). Instead of denying your differences

or hiding behind them in soul-destroying jobs, you'll learn from this book how to follow the beat of your own drummer and still earn a living in the real world.

- *Simplify Your Life*, by Elaine St. James (Hyperion, 1994): Normally, such little books of pithy wisdom are nothing more than expensive stocking stuffers. But this one is different because its sentiments are real, and its stories resonate with common sense and humour.

WHAT I LEARNED ON PELEE ISLAND

1. Don't drive fast.
2. When you try to leave the rat race, you run the risk of being run over or ridiculed by the very people who profess that they want to do the same thing.
3. Don't prejudge people. A closed mind is a closed heart.
4. Always pack a map and a corkscrew.
5. Don't let the pouting of other people — even family members — deter you from achieving your heart's desires.

6. Wear thick work socks.

7. Get to know your neighbours. They are your lifeline, and you never know when you'll need them. Since they live in the same neighbourhood, you already have one thing in common with them.

8. Weed your social garden. If your friends are using you as only a shoulder to cry on, then it's time to part company. Seek out people who are upbeat and effervescent, who are a joy to be around.

9. In all your communications — in person, by e-mail, by phone, by snail mail — be mindful of what you say and how you express it. Be careful not to leave the wrong impression. Often you get only one chance.

10. Sometimes your mom is right (but only sometimes).

11. Don't fight back. Doing so only antagonizes your opponent, inflames the argument, and ultimately solves nothing. Make humble pie a staple of your diet. When you humbly accept the blame, you diffuse your opponent's need to blame you, and suddenly you come out the winner.

12. Go out on a school night.

13. Wave to everyone you see, and say hello to strangers.

14. Should'ves, could'ves, and would'ves don't count for anything.

15. Fast food is the scourge of diets and pocketbooks.

16. Distant places, even smaller places, have the same problems and petty politics as big cities.

17. Don't discount the richness of life that smaller towns and cities can offer you. They are untapped and unheralded places to work, live, and raise your children.
18. Let yourself be guided by your instincts. When God wants to teach you a truth, he plants it in your instinct, not in your intellect.
19. Move slowly.
20. Always show flexibility and forgiveness in your dealings with others. You never know when you'll need someone to return the favour.
21. Give yourself an annual review. It will clarify who you are and where you are going. Repeat the favourite stories of your life often to affirm your identity.
22. There really is a God.

ZOË'S DIARY

January 7, 2001

Today, I am leaving for Pelee Island! Our plane ride is at 3 p.m. I've got the addresses of all my friends so I can write to them. I think I packed everything I need. I feel a bit like Anne of Green Gables because I am going to an island. I feel sad because I won't be able to see my dad for a few months, but I am excited to have a new adventure.

The Pelee Project

January 8, 2001

Today was my first day at Pelee Island Public School. Was I ever nervous! Mom dropped me off in front of the school and said: "OK, Zoë, go inside, and meet your teachers by yourself." I said: "Mom!!" She said that she was just kidding. I knew she was (sort of). The school is really small: It has three classrooms and one office. We met Mrs. N. She was the teacher for Grade 6, 7, and 8, and I think she was also the principal. She took us to Mr. Galloway's room. He teaches Grades 3 and 5, but not 4, because there weren't any. I thought that was pretty weird: No Grade 4s on the entire island! Mr. Galloway teaches Math and English. There are four Grade 5s, and they were all boys. I guess it won't be that bad because all the Grade 6s are girls. By the afternoon, I did make some Grade 6 friends. At the end of the day, I took the school bus home. Mom was waiting for me inside the house. Today was a pretty good day.

January 22, 2001

Today is Mom's birthday. For her birthday, I bought her a little china typewriter that opens up so you can put something small inside, and a snow globe with loons inside it. I hope she likes them. I bought them both at Dick Holl's Trading Post. The Trading Post is a very interesting shop, with lots of rooms crammed full of knickknacks and clothes. It's so full of stuff that you almost trip over everything. I could spend hours in there. It would take that long just to look at everything. After dinner, Mom and I played a game of Scrabble, and I actually won! I was surprised because usually Mom wins.

February 10, 2001

Today, my class with Mrs. N. held a Valentine's Tea at the Legion. We set some tables, made a lot of tea, and put out all the baked goodies that we all made — or that our parents made. At 2 p.m., people started to arrive, and we escorted them to the tables. Each guest was given a valentine with a number on it. One of the girls collected the portion of the valentine ticket that had the guest's name on it. Mom had #42. A few people won the first few prizes. The next prize was some red candles — and Mom's name was drawn! I gave Mom the box of candles. She said that her two lucky numbers are 4 and 2.

February 24, 2001

Today was Saturday, and Mom and I went to the Legion for movie day. During the winter, they show movies for the island's kids, but it's not like a theatre: They just play a video on the Legion's TV. Today it was *Willie Wonka and the Chocolate Factory*. Some of the kids from school were there. One of the moms who was there was a woman who called Mom an unkind name on the Web. I didn't want to go when I heard she was there. But Mom said we had to. Mom went over and introduced herself to the lady. They talked, but they didn't yell. I don't like people saying unkind things about my mom.

March 12, 2001

On Pelee Island, there are two kids who live with their dad and their stepmom on the weekends. Their names are Kaeleigh and Kieran. Kieran was born on the exact same day as me, October 2, 1990, but he was born earlier in the day than me. We went to Billy Hill's house to feed his cats. Billy Hill is an old man who lives in a nursing home on the mainland during the winter, but his summer home is just down the road from where we are living. Beside his house is a really old house that he used to live in. It's a wreck. Now only his cats live there. He had about 20 cats! (I think he has only about 10 cats now.) It was neat to see the cats crawl out from under the house to get the food. The cats were very shy, and if you came close they would just run away. Kaeleigh, Kieran and I played a lot, especially in their backyard because it's humongous! We usually played Cops and Robbers.

March 14, 2001

Today is paczki (pronounced pounchkey) day at the Legion. Kaeleigh was there with me. Paczkis are fun to make. You get some dough and put jelly in the middle. Then you fry them in oil. After that, you can roll them in sugar or cinnamon. I made the ultimate paczki by rolling it in sugar *and* cinnamon! It was good! Even though it is a little hard to make paczkis, they are worth it!

March 16, 2001

Today, Dad came to visit me on the island. (I saved him a paczki or two!) I was really worried about him getting here because there was a really big storm. I felt sick on the ferry over to Leamington, where we were going to meet him. But he arrived on time, and he and I took the ferry back to Pelee. It was a smoother trip. When we got there, I showed Dad Vin Villa, and we saw birds, such as the eastern meadow lark, the horned lark, and the killdeer. I also showed him my school, and the "downtown." After that, we went to our home and watched TV. He made me his famous potatoes for dinner. They're sooooo good! My dad said he has been to the island before, and I think he had a good time. I can't wait to see him again, which will probably be in April.

March 31, 2001

It was the Hillbilly Hoedown at the Legion tonight. Irma (the owner of the house we are living in) came to the island that day. The Hillbilly Hoedown is a celebration of the last Legion get-together before the tourism season starts. I dressed up as Casey Eastwood — the daughter of Clint Eastwood. Mo, the nurse on the island, won a candle holder and $105. She donated $25 to the Pelee community. Mo is my friend. I like her because she's crazy and cool! I didn't win anything, but that's OK. All my friends from school were there, and we played on the ice-covered rocks by the lake. I don't think Mom would have liked to know about that! We also played tag.

April 6, 2001

Today is a P.D. Day. Thank God! Mom and I went to Fish Point. I really wanted to go because I knew we wouldn't have any more chances to go since it was our last week. I also wanted to be able to tell my friends that I had been to the most southerly inhabited point in Canada.

April 13, 2001

We are leaving Pelee Island today. At my school yesterday, Mr. Galloway made a card and everybody signed it. I will keep it forever. We had a good-bye ritual with Mary-Lou on the beach. Mary-Lou was dressed really colourfully. The good-bye ritual was a little sad because I won't get to see the people I met here for a long time, but on the other hand, I will be able to see the other friends I left behind. So I am excited that I will be going back to Hamilton. Living on Pelee Island for three months is an experience I won't forget.

April 17, 2001

Today is my first day back to school in Hamilton! I was so excited because I missed my friends so much. The first friend I saw was Elise. She took me to all my other friends. Emma was particularly excited to see me. Not a lot of my friends asked me questions about my stay on Pelee Island. I wonder why that is? One of them said that her mom went to Pelee Island and Point Pelee. I asked which one she went to. The girl said that she went to both because they are the same thing! I wanted to tell her she was wrong, but I thought, "Forget it." Besides that, my first day back was great!